**A+Awards 2016
Archititzer**

A+Awards 2016
Archititzer

About Architizer and the A+Awards

6

The Architizer A+Awards Book

7

Jury and Popular Choice Winners

9

Index

238

About Architizer and the A+Awards

With portfolios from over 40,000 architecture firms worldwide, Architizer is the premier online destination for architects. The site features a browsable database of 120,000+ buildings, an online magazine covering industry news and insights and, introduced in 2016, a products marketplace that enables architects to build better.

Architizer has long been familiar with connecting the world's best architecture and interiors with the products behind them. In its fourth year, the annual A+Awards is the largest global program for both architectural and product design.

The History of the Awards
Launched in 2013, the A+Awards consists of three core areas.

Typology — While architects do many things, at the core of our profession we make buildings and spaces. These categories celebrate traditional building types, ranging from residential, office, and commercial to transportation, landscape, and cultural.

Plus — These awards are designed to showcase how architects build relationships. They celebrate the intersection of architecture and light, art, communication, and more. New in 2016, the Plus categories also include unbuilt projects and conceptual designs.

Product — Every architect and interior designer knows that it takes spectacular products and materials to make their vision a reality. We are proud to present products that speak to the solutions that matter most to architects.

The Jury
Comprised of 300+ luminaries across architecture and other industries, our jury includes both the people who make buildings and the people who help make great buildings happen. Each category has a Popular Choice winner in addition to the Jury winner, with hundreds of thousands of design enthusiasts and professionals voting for their favorites from around the globe.

The Trophy
Architizer has teamed up with Brooklyn-based studio Snarkitecture to create a bespoke trophy design for the A+Awards. Like the program itself, Snarkitecture is concerned with the intersections of design and function, as well as architecture and society. Starting as Styrofoam, the statuette undergoes a series of casting phases before becoming a cube of cultured marble with a hairline crack along its equator. This trophy, which splits in half to reveal a black "+" rising from a micro-landscape of contours, proves to be as dynamic as the A+Awards as a whole.

The Architizer A+Awards Book

This book celebrates the world's best architecture, but you don't have to take my word for it. These winners were chosen by an international jury of over 300 experts and endorsed by hundreds of thousands of votes online. Our entrants, from more than one hundred countries, run the gamut of architectural typology and form, from the tallest towers to the most elaborate and refined cultural centers.

The A+Awards were designed to fill a void in the architecture award universe: to create an award that isn't just for one annual winner, but to celebrate all of the amazing buildings that get built in a year. To create that award, one substantive enough to resonate on a global scale, we partnered with innovators in multiple fields: The *Wall Street Journal Magazine* to get our winners in front of global decision makers; The Webby Awards to create a robust and inclusive judging program; and of course Phaidon, to make this beautiful book possible.

At Architizer we stop at nothing to create innovative programs for architects. That is why I am so excited to launch Architizer Source this year—the world's first marketplace for building products. Architizer Source unleashes the intrinsic value of what architects do—in the U.S., architects control more than $570 billion in construction each year—and with Source they will be better able to address their project needs.

As an architect I know that there is so much that technology can do for the way architects work. Register for Architizer Source at arc.ht/phaidon-aplus and join us as we revolutionize the way buildings get built.

— Marc Kushner

Jury and Popular Choice Winners

Awards Category **Typology** / Type **Residential: Apartment** / Winner **Jury**

Pivot New York, NY, USA

Emphasizing open space, the custom cabinetry in this redesigned prewar studio creates separate spaces for multifunctionality.

Pivot is a prewar studio designed by Architecture Workshop PC, based out of Brooklyn. The brief called for hosting ten for dinner, sleeping six, a private study, and an efficient kitchen for a client that loves to entertain, all within a 400-square-foot studio apartment. The project emphasizes open space while overlaying multifunctionality, transforming in response to changing needs.

Extensive custom cabinetry creates various spatial experiences depending on use, ranging from serene white walls to lush wood interiors. The layout capitalizes on a preexisting wall-bed nook to generate an unfolding bedroom concealed behind a pivoting wall. Residents come home to an airy modern apartment where everything has its place.

Many elements of the design are multifunctional. Pivoting a large wall cabinet filled with storage creates two separate spaces that can be used independently when needed, in the process revealing a wall bed with a window that provides daylight to the inner room. A sofa unfolds allowing guests to sleep in their own private room. The kitchen features a backsplash that lifts to reveal storage space. A compact washroom feels like a spa with a double sink and a folding glass door that forms a minimalist shower.

Status
Built

Year
2013

Firm
Architecture Workshop PC

Firm location
Brooklyn, NY, USA

Awards Category Typology / Type **Residential: Apartment** / Winner **Popular Choice**

Nevern Square Apartment London, UK

In this contemporary reinterpretation of the British Edwardian two-room layout, a wide, glazed internal opening gives the front and rear rooms an extraordinary visual depth and continuity.

Located on the raised ground floor of a late-nineteenth-century Edwardian terrace building, the project for the Nevern Square Apartment has been conceived to turn a 740-square-foot, self-contained flat—old-fashioned and very fragmented as a result of a poor 1970s conversion—into a comfortable and fully equipped apartment.

The design concept is based on the contemporary reinterpretation of the British Edwardian two-room layout, with one big room at the front and one at the rear. It both reveals the original rooms' proportions and enhances the two beautiful windows at the front.

It is the intersection between the two spaces that generates the element that makes this project unique: a wide, glazed internal opening that gives the front and rear rooms an extraordinary visual depth and continuity, and that can be screened when needed. This opening works like an additional big window inside the house, allowing natural daylight during the whole day, saving considerable energy, and giving the impression that both the living area and the master bedroom double face (front and rear) the external spaces, with a beautiful view to the leafy Nevern Square gardens.

Status
Built

Year
2014

Firm
Daniele Petteno Architecture Workshop

Firm location
London, UK

Awards Category Typology / Type Residential: Private House XS / Winner Jury

Colorado Outward Bound School Micro Cabins Leadville, CO, USA

Microdormitories for the Colorado Outward Bound School in Denver, these tiny cabins hover above the landscape, offering views of the surrounding forest and mountain range.

Located on a steep hillside in a pine forest, the Micro Cabins in Leadville, Colorado, were designed as microdormitories for the Colorado Outward Bound School by the Colorado Building Workshop in Denver. The cabins sit lightly on the landscape, directing views from private spaces towards trees, rock outcroppings, and distant mountain views of the Mosquito Range.

To satisfy the clients' lodging and storage requirements, and to facilitate completion in three weeks of on-site construction, the cabins were conceived as two separate elements: a "box" and a "frame." The frame acts as a storage device for the educators' large gear while simultaneously housing the cabin box and covered porches. The prefabricated cabin box rests in the frame under the protection of a snow roof designed to keep the winter snow load off the waterproofed roof below. Hot-rolled steel provides a low maintenance rain screen for the box. This steel cladding and the vertical columns blend with the forest minimizing, the visual impact of the cabins.

The interior of the cabin is skinned in CNC'd birch plywood, bringing warmth to the interior and evoking a connection with the trees surrounding the site.

Status
Built

Year
2015

Firm
Colorado Building Workshop/ University of Colorado Denver

Firm location
Denver, CO, USA

Awards Category **Typology** / Type **Residential: Private House XS** / Winner **Popular Choice**

Rainforest Retreat Vancouver Island, BC, Canada

A long slim structure—to minimize the impact of the building on the site and to provide the client with both a home and an art studio—this retreat is nestled in tall woods, allowing for intimacy and shelter.

Located on the coast of Vancouver Island, British Columbia, this small dwelling provides the client with a retreat to call home and an art studio in which to work. The retreat is nestled in tall woods, allowing for intimate, individually framed views of the old forest. The 825-square-foot space contains a kitchen, a living/art studio, one bathroom, one bedroom, and a private deck.

    The client's wishes for simplicity, gentle exterior appearance, a small footprint, and abundant natural light set the stage for an open sculptural form. Great effort was taken to minimize the building's impact on the site, resulting in a long, slim structure. Slightly twisting two main blocks of the plan, and overlapping these shapes, made a building modest in area ever expansive and full of unexpected depth. The roof members were exposed, giving homage to the natural environment. In the shade of the trees, all that was required for cooling were operable windows at low and high reaches creating constant fresh air movement. Custom lighting was designed to enhance the forest experience on rainy or dark days. And a periscope light acts as a beacon guiding the client safely to their parking spot.

Status
Built

Year
2014

Firm
AGATHOM

Firm location
Toronto, ON, Canada

Awards Category **Typology** / Type **Residential: Private House M** / Winner **Jury**

Villa Schoorl Schoorl, The Netherlands

Villa Schoorl, nestled in a beautiful dune landscape, is a modern interpretation of a typical farm, coated in black metal and with rolled steel and light maple interiors.

In the middle of a beautiful dune landscape in the Netherlands lies Schoorl, a small village surrounded by serene nature and magnificent views. At the end of one of the many avenues with high trees, a dark silhouette has risen. Villa Schoorl, designed by studio PROTOTYPE, is a modern interpretation of a typical farm as a family residence.

The outer shell is black metal, a combination of anodized aluminum for the side facades and roof, and a one-piece rolled steel plate for the front facade.

The succession of volumes within the silhouette of a typical Dutch house is the starting point for the spatial concept. Depending on the different functions the volumes were designed in a more open or closed manner. The volumes were then modified to form a succession of open, closed, light, and dark spaces. In between these volumes, a central, open living area connects to the veranda where the exterior flows into the interior.

The interior volumes are again made of with rolled steel, in contrast to surrounding spaces where light maple wood is used.

Status
Built

Year
2015

Firm
studio PROTOTYPE

Firm location
Amsterdam, The Netherlands

Awards Category Typology / Type **Residential: Private House M** / Winner **Popular Choice**

Casa Candelaria San Miguel de Allende, Mexico

On the outskirts of San Miguel de Allende, Casa Candelaria is built of rammed earth walls using the soil from the actual site to integrate the house with the environment, emphasizing that the main element outside of the house is the vegetation.

Casa Candelaria is located on the outskirts of San Miguel de Allende, Mexico. It was conceived around the concept of strength of presence and belonging to the site where it is built. It was decided to return to the program of the Mexican haciendas and arrange the new house around courtyards.

Another key intention for the design development was the construction method. The decision to use rammed earth walls using the soil from the actual site along with the addition of natural dyes to achieve the black tone seeks to integrate the house with the environment, emphasizing that the main element outside of the house is the vegetation.

The benefit of using rammed earth walls is the added insulation. The thick walls allow the house to be cool in hot daytime temperatures and warm at night when the temperature of San Miguel tends to fall drastically. Using materials extracted from the site itself resulted in considerable savings on materials and transportation, making the construction time and cost effective.

This house responds to a contemporary Mexican hacienda using an innovative and effective construction system.

Status
Under Construction

Year
2016

Firm
Cherem, arqs

Firm location
Miami, FL, USA

Awards Category **Typology** / Type **Residential: Private House L** / Winner **Jury**

Choy House Queens, NY, USA

A design for three homes under one roof in Queens, New York City, was the prompt for O'Neill Rose Architects' Choy House.

The client asked O'Neill Rose Architects, based in Brooklyn, to build a home for himself, his wife, and two small children, as well as his younger brother and his wife, and their mother. The challenge was to design three homes under one roof in a neighborhood of Queens, New York, that is defined by single-family homes. Choy House is essentially three disparate dwellings with areas of connection and overlap that reflect the client's familial relationships.

Status
Built

Year
2014

Firm
O'Neill Rose Architects

Firm location
Brooklyn, NY, USA

Awards Category **Typology** / Type **Residential: Private House L** / Winner **Popular Choice**

The Greja House Singapore

Rather than defining space with walls, the rooms of the Greja House are composed of interconnected voids, providing an environment that bonds a family through increased domestic interactions.

This project revisits the fundamental role of a home, providing an environment that bonds a family. The design aims to heighten the occupants' sensorial awareness and to increase domestic interactions. To that end, the spaces were interpreted as a flow. Key to the idea of flow are gestures of connection and circulation, which inform the way the spaces are composed.

Departing from the conventional approach, where walls are used to define space, the rooms are composed of interconnected voids. The way the house interfaces with the lush foreground was achieved by composing basic geometric elements, infused with voids to detach from its boundary.

This matrix of borderless spaces is a white translucent box. Functionally, it acts as a screen that brings filtered daylight into the house while maintaining a degree of privacy. Architecturally, it creates a permeable skin that not only dissolves the boundary between inside and outside but also defines the visual character of the house.

The 3D tapestry of this semi-detached house creates spaces that actively open up domestic dialogue, increasing the opportunities for interaction and enriching the daily activities of its inhabitants.

Status
Built

Year
2014

Firm
Park + Associates

Firm location
Singapore

Awards Category **Typology** / Type **Residential: Private House XL** / Winner **Jury**

Cornwall Gardens Singapore

Around an open space filled with plants and bodies of water are living spaces for a multigenerational family, offering an eco-friendly gathering place lush with a dynamic biodiversity.

Cornwall Gardens, designed by CHANG Architects in Singapore, is intended for multigenerational living.

With a central open space, family and nature share the same breathing room. Plants, bodies of water, and living spaces are integrated as one. The setting provides daylight, natural ventilation, and passive cooling. It offers an eco-friendly environment that promotes general wellness for all.

In the courtyard an old retaining wall with a history of leakage has been transformed into a green outdoor space with a waterfall. Working with the existing terrain, planters for tropical fruit trees cool the air and water and insulate the interiors. The landscaped decks and cascading planters frame the pool and ponds. These also serve as the catchment areas for rainwater, which is recycled for irrigation.

This house has become a popular gathering place for extended family and friends, and has also attracted a range of biodiversity, from bees and butterflies to squirrels.

By keeping its residents constantly in touch with nature, Cornwall Gardens offers fresh definitions of living in the tropics.

Status
Built

Year
2014

Firm
CHANG Architects

Firm location
Singapore

Awards Category **Typology** / Type **Residential: Private House XL** / Winner **Popular Choice**

OVD 919 Cape Town, South Africa

The layout of this concrete residence is designed to mitigate seasonal winds while maximizing the iconic views offered by the steep site.

The brief was to create a contemporary open-plan home on a dramatic site. In response, the house was shifted eastward, allowing the main level to be complemented with sun-facing outdoor terraces and gardens, and maximizing the iconic views toward Robben Island.

There was a need to mitigate seasonal winds. These climatic influences suggested the creation of a series of interlinking rooms that facilitate and promote the indoor-outdoor lifestyle of the region.

Set below Lion's Head, the steep property shares its southern boundary with a national park. Consequently, a decision was made to restrict the four-level building to two stories above the ridge. With limited walls and columns, the top stories appear to float on light, glazed facades. Support spaces are positioned on lower levels, concealed from the road below by a north-facing green wall integrated into the landscape.

All off-shutter concrete was cast using a customized white concrete mix. Once cured, this was sandblasted to reveal a fine, carefully selected aggregate, resulting in a robust look devoid of artifice. Inside, a ribbed pre-cast concrete soffit creates continuity between the internal and external living spaces, with all services carefully coordinated to disappear within the recessed spaces.

Status
Built

Year
2014

Firm
SAOTA

Firm location
Cape Town, South Africa

Awards Category **Typology** / Type **Residential: Multi Unit Housing — Low Rise** / Winner **Jury**

The Great Wall of WA (The Musterers' Quarters) WA, Australia

In a remote cattle station in North Western Australia, the rammed earth–made Great Wall of WA is comprised of twelve compact and energy-efficient units.

The Great Wall of WA (The Musterers' Quarters), designed by Luigi Rosselli Architects based out of Surry Hills, Australia, is located on a remote cattle station in North Western Australia. The rugged, sunburned landscape created an unusual set of design parameters in this project, which provides accommodation for workers during cattle mustering periods. Twelve compact and functional units, both maintenance-free and energy efficient, were needed.

To stabilize the ambient temperatures of the accommodation, the units were placed beneath an existing sand dune and faced with a continuous rammed earth wall. The structures are predominantly not exposed to the sun's heat and are protected from cyclonic conditions. The sand dune arches around the back of the homestead and the Musterers' Quarters fan out toward the view of ghost gum trees scattered on the river banks.

On the highest point a "chapel" dominates the project; a multipurpose room imbued with the sacred aura of the place, from the original indigenous caretakers of the site to the headstones marking the graves of the first settlers at the bottom of the hill. The Chapel is a simple oval plan with a skewed conical Corten steel roof that provides protection from the sun.

Status
Built

Year
2014

Firm
Luigi Rosselli Architects

Firm location
Surry Hills, Australia

Awards Category **Typology** / Type **Residential: Multi Unit Housing — Low Rise** / Winner **Popular Choice**

The Afsharians' House Kermanshah, Iran

The clients wished to be able to convert the house into separate apartment units for their children in the future, requiring flexibility in both plan and facade.

Architect-designed houses may be compared to abstract and conceptual paintings. The Afsharians' house, in Kermanshah, Iran, is a three-story building belonging to a couple and their children.

Since the clients' request was to provide each of their children with a single, separate unit in the future, the building was designed to be converted from a home into apartments. This demand required a flexibility in plan and facade that challenged the architect to find a solution that could look adequate for the present and still look elegant and well-proportioned after the extension.

Accordingly, taking building height and width into account, ReNa designed a bold square shape with a crack in it, converting the building into a sculpture emerging from the street. This solution not only exposes the entrance very well, but also responds to the upper-level space divisions in a convenient way.

Status
Built

Year
2014

Firm
ReNa Design

Firm location
Tehran, Iran

Awards Category **Typology** / Type **Residential: Multi Unit Housing — Mid Rise** / Winner **Jury & Popular Choice**

Highpark Monterrey, Mexico

On the outskirts of Monterrey, Highpark is a ten-level apartment building, adapted to the intense sun thanks to shifting floor plates and a cool facade made with local stone.

Highpark is located on the outskirts of the northern city of Monterrey, Mexico. Surrounded by the majestic Sierra Madre Oriental mountain range, the project was designed to take full advantage of its geographic location.

The building is integrated into the pedestrian realm, a recurring design concern for Rojkind Arquitectos, based out of Mexico City. Residents and visitors alike can enjoy the shaded outdoor space.

In order to mitigate the intense sun, the flootprints shift from floor to floor, playing a game of light and shadow. The use of local stone on the facade keeps the building cool and creates a dynamic appearance that changes as the sun moves across the horizon.

Highpark consists of a total of ten levels, as well as three and a half levels of underground parking. The first two levels are for commercial retail, and the remaining eight levels are for luxury apartments with recreational and entertainment spaces including a pool, a gym, and a spa.

Status
Built

Year
2015

Firm
Rojkind Arquitectos

Firm location
Mexico City, Mexico

Awards Category **Typology** / Type **Residential: Multi Unit Housing — High Rise** / Winner **Jury**

SkyTerrace@Dawson Singapore

Bordering the Alexandra Canal Linear Park in Singapore, this residential project addresses strong connectivity to its surrounding greenery and extended framework for housing multi-generational families.

SkyTerrace@Dawson is located in Dawson Estate, Singapore, and is designed by SCDA Architects Singapore. Running along the site's southern boundary is the Alexandra Canal Linear Park. The project is composed of five residential forty- to forty-three-story towers and a four-story parking lot. The towers and parking lot are connected by sky bridges at every level, enabling residents to enjoy an uninterrupted journey from the parking lots to their apartments.

The design embodies three key ideas: housing in a park, connectivity to surroundings, and multigenerational living.

In response to the first two key ideas, the project site has seamless connectivity to greenery on three sides. This green concept is expanded further by introducing lush landscaping on the ground plane that travels up the building facades in the form of green terracing, roof gardens, and green sky terraces between the towers. The third design idea enables multigenerational living by providing the spatial framework for extended families to occupy interconnected loft units.

The project features sustainable design technologies like drip irrigation, rainwater harvesting, bio-retention basins, and solar energy systems. SkyTerrace@Dawson is a Green Mark Platinum project and received the PUB ABC Water Certification.

Status
Built

Year
2015

Firm
SCDA Architects Singapore

Firm location
Singapore

Awards Category **Typology & Plus** / Type **Residential: Multi Unit Housing — High Rise, Architecture + Concrete** / Winner **Jury & Popular Choice**

170 Amsterdam New York, NY, USA

A dynamic, glass exoskeleton wraps around a building with projecting slabs and columns that create a brise-soleil effect while providing floor-to-ceiling windows for the apartments within.

170 Amsterdam's exoskeleton is derived from its location at the intersection of Central Park, the Lincoln Towers green, the muscular buildings of lower Amsterdam Avenue and Lincoln Center, and the ornate buildings of the Upper West Side with their heavy rustications.

The design responds to this unique location by moving the structure to the outside. The structure has a lightness of expression when viewed directly, but also a solidity when seen obliquely, providing a deep facade connecting the building to its context. The projecting slabs and columns provide a brise-soleil effect and shade the all-glass facade.

At ground level, the columns create a dynamic street wall, with the exposed structure angling into the sidewalk. At the top, the exoskeleton continues beyond the roof supporting a canopy for the sky terrace. The structure and the facade act as one, giving the building a tectonic and physical presence.

Inside, the exposed concrete columns angle through the public spaces piercing the floors and walls of the lobby and common spaces. In the apartments, seeing the structure through the floor-to-ceiling glass has the effect of being suspended, while the unbroken window-line expands the size of the small apartments.

Status
Built

Year
2015

Firm
Handel Architects

Firm location
New York, NY, USA

Awards Category Typology / Type **Residential: Residential Interiors** / Winner **Jury**

Jerry House Chaam Beach, Thailand

Minimal circulation for a high-energy family is the central focus for Jerry House, where layers of nets offer an alternative mode of moving around the space.

Jerry House is a holiday home in Chaam Beach, Thailand. The architects of onion, based out of Bangkok, created a space where minimal circulation is the norm and family members are encouraged to play.

Running, climbing, hiding, hanging, and even falling are the proposed physical activities, exceeding the boundaries of the everyday.

Central to the designers' concern is the linkage of passageways. Onion adds an extra set of vertical circulations at the central hallway and uses customized nets to build five layers of horizontal planes of different slopes, heights, and sizes. The nets act almost like extensions of the floors. Each layer of net has a hole and each hole is set in a different location. Children and adults can climb up the metal ladders from the ground floor to one of the kids' bedrooms on the third floor. When they look upward, the mirrored film attached to the ceiling gives the illusion that the players are floating in the air, and that the overlapping layers of net are higher than they actually are.

Status
Built

Year
2014

Firm
onion

Firm location
Bangkok, Thailand

Awards Category Typology / Type Residential: Residential Interiors / Winner Popular Choice

Skygarden House Toronto, ON, Canada

Maximizing useable outdoor spaces on multiple levels addresses the owners' desire for a better connection to the home's natural surroundings and extends the living surface.

Situated on a narrow lot in an older Toronto neighborhood, the Skygarden House provides outdoor living spaces on multiple levels to address the owners' desire for a better connection to the home's natural surroundings.

Although the new house is only 2,420 square feet, it feels much larger. The rooms expand beyond the interior to a series of highly useable outdoor spaces that enrich the domestic experience. The plants were selected to provide visual interest year round. Even the existing porch at the front of the house is remade into a private outdoor dining room, enclosed by a five-foot-high wood screen, extending the private realm into the public arena. On the third floor, two significant outdoor spaces provide green respite. An exposed roof deck at the back of the house has plentiful views over the neighborhood and into the extensive green canopy surrounding the house. At the front of the house, half of the master bedroom is given over to an intimate exterior space clad in warm ash, with a recessed planter and an opening carved into the roof for natural light, access to rainwater, and ample views of green.

Status
Built

Year
2015

Firm
DUBBELDAM Architecture + Design

Firm location
Toronto, ON, Canada

Awards Category **Typology** / Type **Residential: Unbuilt Residential** / Winner **Jury**

High Living Mumbai, India

High Living is a proposed housing solution for the dense Dharavi slum in Mumbai, featuring lateral connectivity and the introduction of large green spaces to this part of the city.

The extreme population density of Dharavi, one of the largest slums in the world, produces two opposing features; one is the unique locality and dynamic energy of this part of the greater Mumbai urban fabric, and the other is the problem of public health and safety. The area's lack of infrastructure, complicated ownership, illegal settlement, and poverty have made many previous conventional redevelopment efforts into cosmetic dreams. Responding to this problem, the prefabricated connected towers of High Living can provide a radical but realistic cure.

The towers have multiple connections to provide lateral stability, creating an arch shape. One exoskeleton frame holds eight containers, and all structural loads go through these frames—not the stacking of containers.

High Living provides multiple egress routes, since the towers share the means of egress with each other. The large bridge area, created by structural need, will be a generous public park, unprecedented in a slum. This system can grow slowly to expand the elevated green and free the ground for the next phase of urban planning. All units have generous outdoor balconies; water and air are controlled by the concentrated tower system.

Status
Concept

Firm
Dioinno Architecture

Firm location
Buffalo, NY, USA

Awards Category **Typology** / Type **Residential: Unbuilt Residential** / Winner **Popular Choice**

Golden Ratio Ghent, Belgium

This project aims to integrate four luxury apartments and an exclusive store in the heart of medieval Ghent, restoring the balance of the golden ratio in a rare historic context.

In the heart of medieval Ghent, a heartless building dislocated a nineteenth-century street. This project aimed to integrate four luxury apartments and an exclusive store, plus restore balance in a rare historic context. Most nineteenth-century cityscapes were conceived around the principle of the golden ratio, not only in the proportions of their buildings but also in street width.

Instead of copying or abstracting the grids of historic facades, Govaert & Vanhoutte Architectuurburo went back to the core principles of the golden ratio to create our own purified grid. It remains linked to the preexisting one. Further, adding stacked concrete frames underlines the proportions but also creates massiveness. Inside the frames, lucid glass boxes determine inside and outside space, both horizontal and vertical.

Status
Under Construction

Year
2017

Firm
Govaert & Vanhoutte Architectuurburo

Firm location
Brugge, Belgium

Awards Category Typology / Type Commercial: Office — Low Rise / Winner Jury

TERMEH Office — Retail Building Hamedan, Iran

TERMEH Office challenges the skills of the architects in drawing formal connections between the building and the street, as well as within the building itself.

TERMEH Office by Farshad Mehdizadeh + Ahmad Bathaei is located in Hamedan, one of Iran's historical cities. Hamedan has active urban space characterized by squares and an important north-south urban axis connecting them. This axis crosses the site's western side. The brief called for a two-floor building with commercial functions, including a retail ground floor and a private office on the first floor.

Since this project has different functions on each floor, the idea was to connect the functions separately but directly to the urban space. Furthermore, the architects needed a vertical access solution. This solution was in the form of a separator slab which became stairs to connect the office directly to the walkway in front. The roof was given over to the office as a roof garden for business ceremonies and outdoor parties. The facade is a continuous system made of local bricks patterned with local and traditional techniques. This facade was made with openings to control the light.

Status
Built

Year
2015

Firm
Farshad Mehdizadeh + Ahmad Bathaei

Firm location
Tehran, Iran

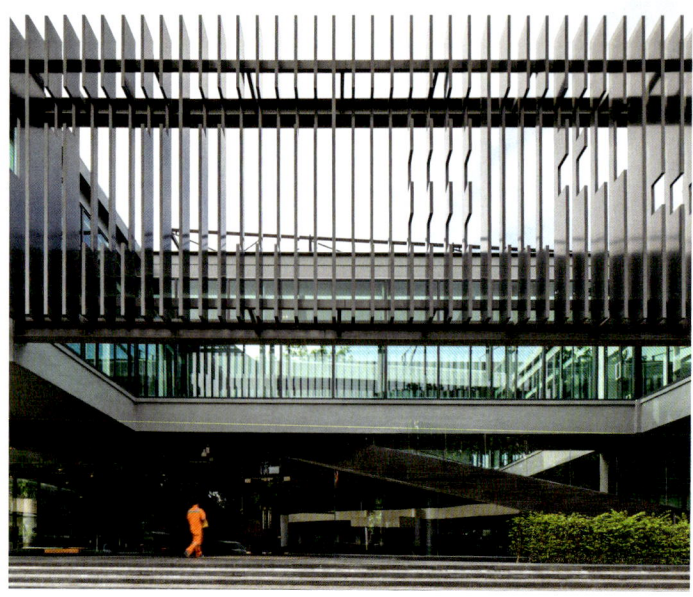

Awards Category Typology / Type Commercial: Office — Low Rise / Winner Popular Choice

PTTEP-S1 Office Lan Krabue, Thailand

Concrete slabs, married with grass-covered surfaces, make the setting for the main office for PTTEP's Sirikit oil field site in Thailand.

PTT Exploration and Production Public Company Limited (PTTEP) is a national petroleum exploration and production company in Thailand, dedicated to providing a sustainable petroleum supply to the country. The Sirikit oil field site has been in operation for 30 years. In 2011, PTTEP held a competition to design a two-story office building to commemorate this 30-year history. PTTEP wanted to build a 21,500-square-foot building as a main office for the site. The space under the ground plane, which is made of folded concrete slabs and covered with grass, can be used as an entrance to the building. This space also houses other programs such as a lecture room and reception area.

The top of the new, folded ground plane can also be used as a flexible space. While it can be used as a stair during the day, it can also be turned into a performance space during events.

Status
Built

Year
2014

Firm
OfficeAT

Firm location
Bangkok, Thailand

Awards Category Typology / Type Commercial: Office — Mid Rise / Winner Jury

Shinsegae International Seoul, South Korea

Designed to meet Korea's progressive energy codes, this building's skin incorporates a range of technologies to control thermal comfort while maximizing the benefits of natural daylight.

A new icon in the heart of Gangnam-gu, one of Seoul's largest districts, this fifteen-story building by Seattle architects Olsun Kindig unites more than 500 Shinsegae employees who had previously been spread among several buildings throughout the city. The project includes staff offices and meeting spaces, design studios, a rooftop garden and sculpture park, and ground-level retail and restaurant spaces that face onto a public plaza.

Movement and materiality are particularly evident within the building's first four floors, where seven custom eight-foot-diameter steel wheels open and close thirty-five-foot-tall external panels to modulate daylight. The dynamic ethos of the fashion world is captured in these kinetic components.

The high-performance, custom-designed facade is a direct response to the client's desire for a corporate flagship that departs from the traditional look of modern commercial buildings. Designed to meet Korea's progressive energy codes, the building's skin incorporates a range of technologies that reduce heat gain while optimizing thermal comfort and maximizing natural daylight. Each component of the gridded facade contributes to the structural fidelity of the building as much as to its unique aesthetic, evoking a sense of woven material or tapestry.

Status
Built

Year
2015

Firm
Olson Kundig

Firm location
Seattle, WA, USA

Awards Category **Typology** / Type **Commercial: Office — Mid Rise** / Winner **Popular Choice**

JTI Headquarters Geneva, Switzerland

Around a central courtyard and a permeable pedestrian route, a continuous landscape loops throughout the building, connecting disparate programs through social spaces.

Surrounded by extensive parklands, the new headquarters for JTI (Japan Tobacco International) is located in a Geneva district home to many other prestigious international organizations.

The opposing corners of the building's form are elevated, creating a central courtyard and a permeable pedestrian route through the site, with access to a local transport hub. A continuous landscape loops throughout the building—from the lobby to the top floor—connecting offices, meeting rooms, a business center, and an auditorium with the social spaces. The pathway is distinguished by the use of different materials and color palettes, as well as curated installations by internationally renowned artists.

The interior design concept follows the client's desire to create an overall community that could help change the company's business culture from closed-off working environments to a more flexible workplace. The more than 1,000 employees have access to a number of communal areas: a panoramic restaurant, a cafeteria, roof terraces, a courtyard, and informal meeting points.

Bolstered by a host of sustainable features such as a green roof, fresh air intake vents, low-carbon heating and cooling, and a high performance facade, the building ranks among the most sustainable projects in Europe.

Status
Built

Year
2015

Firm
Skidmore, Owings & Merrill

Firm location
San Francisco, CA, USA

Awards Category Typology & Plus / Type Commercial: Retail, Architecture + Glass / Winner Jury

Apple Store — Stanford Palo Alto, CA, USA

Rarely has an Apple store been so visually recognizable and physically accessible as this two-part pavilion-concept store.

Apple Store, Stanford is a two-room pavilion-concept store within Palo Alto's Stanford Shopping Center. It is a fresh direction for Apple's retail program designed, by San Francisco architects Bohlin Cywinski Jackson, reinterpreting many favorite architectural themes the brand has developed over the past thirteen years, such as expansive transparent glass, soft stainless steel, and warm stone.

With 180 lineal feet of storefront glass and three entrances, rarely has an Apple store been so visually recognizable and physically accessible. The transparent front room is made column-free by the integration of slender structural glass fins, with the storefront supporting the roof above. With only wood tables and a stone wall resting on the floor, the space below the roof is left uninhibited for the exploration of products.

As a counterpoint to the transparency and openness of the front room, the back room, which is dedicated to service, training, and accessory retail display, is enclosed and calming.

Delicate stainless steel beams support a gently arcing glass roof that fills the back room with daylight. Extending to surrounding walls, the expansive glass roof allows vertical stone walls to extend unobstructed to the sky above, adding to the perception of being outdoors.

Status
Built

Year
2013

Firm
Bohlin Cywinski Jackson

Firm location
San Francisco, CA, USA

Awards Category **Typology** / Type **Commercial: Office — High Rise** / Winner **Jury & Popular Choice**

TELUS Garden Office Tower Vancouver, BC, Canada

Radically reviving an aging block in downtown Vancouver, this office tower is the first building in Canada to target the 2009 LEED Platinum standard, thanks to energy-producing technologies and major public amenities.

The TELUS Garden Office Tower designed by Henriquez Partners Architects has radically transformed an aging block of downtown Vancouver into a future-friendly community that fuses beauty, functionality, and environmental stewardship. TELUS Garden's 450,000-square-foot office tower, at the southwest corner of West Georgia and Richards streets, is an expansion of the telecommunications giant's existing headquarters.

The signature building is the first in Canada to target the 2009 Leadership in Energy and Environmental Design (LEED) Platinum standard, with features like pavilion rainwater capture, district energy, and solar panels. TELUS Garden is quickly garnering a reputation as a hub for innovation, business, and social activity in the city core.

Public spaces, amenities and art are also major components. The office tower features 14,000 square feet of green roofs growing organic produce for local restaurants, Sky Garden meeting rooms, British Columbia artwork, programmable LED lighting that project colored images, and a media wall where cultural events can be broadcast to the public.

Status
Built

Year
2015

Firm
Henriquez Partners Architects

Firm location
Vancouver, BC, Canada

Awards Category **Typology** / Type **Commercial: Shopping Center** / Winner **Jury**

COEX Seoul, South Korea

COEX, a subterranean retail complex in Seoul, is a piece of urban infrastructure, featuring progressive retail circulation and an extensive architectural language of folded and undulating surfaces.

COEX is a 914,932-square-foot subterranean retail complex located in the Gangnam district of Seoul, South Korea, and designed by the Los Angeles–based firm Gensler. It occupies the subterranean level of a superblock containing Seoul's primary convention center, three hotels, a casino, a performing arts complex, three office towers, and a bus terminal.

COEX is less a mall than a piece of urban infrastructure. Retail circulation was reconfigured to create seamless connections and clear hierarchies between the existing tower lobbies, new and existing public plazas, and the subway stations at both ends of the site.

A new two-level glass pavilion creates a grand interior plaza. The pavilion functions as a new entrance, event space, and crossroads. The plaza is fully sunlit via a glazed undulating roof supported by a space frame that integrates a metal screen panel system for sun control.

Another set of interventions along the eastern edge creates an architectural language of folded and undulating perforated metal panels and fascias for two existing sunken plazas. The white undulating panels are visible from surrounding streets and towers, and create a clear identifiable language for the plazas that permeates the language of the reconfigured interior concourses.

Status
Built

Year
2014

Firm
Gensler

Firm location
Los Angeles, CA, USA

Awards Category **Typology & Plus** / Type **Commercial: Shopping Center** / Winner **Popular Choice**

Kurve 7 Bangkok, Thailand

In a dense residential district of Bangkok, Stu/D/O realizes a new neighborhood commercial space that is linked together by a series of open-air gardens and public spaces around a curved promenade.

Kurve 7 is a mall located within a dense residential district of Bangkok. Using a series of soft curvature strategies to define, frame, lead, and connect, Stu/D/O was able to realize the goal of creating a new neighborhood commercial space linked together by a series of open-air gardens and public spaces.

Due to zoning restrictions, the massing is divided into nine separated blocks with commercial area no larger than 3,200 square feet each. The small commercial blocks are organized into two longitudinal groups in the front and rear, opening up a curved promenade that elongates the corridor space while providing new visual interest. In order to visually link the separated programmatic massing, a continuous curved roof is used to architecturally connect the blocks.

The ground plane at the entry is lifted up to create a gently sloping ramp, connecting the farthest boundary to the center. Together with the curving path, these curves define the main approach and create an intimate space that becomes an open-air amphitheater and garden for the public.

Status
Built

Year
2014

Firm
stu/D/O Architects

Firm location
Bangkok, Thailand

Awards Category **Typology** / Type **Commercial: Retail** / Winner **Popular Choice**

Unilux Beirut, Lebanon

Reinventing a shallow space as a showroom for lighting manufacturer Unilux, SOMA's design is quite literally sculpted by light.

With sixty-five feet of frontage but only thirteen feet of depth, this existing ground-floor space provided a unique opportunity for a commercial street front lighting showroom.

Envisioning the space as a solid mass, SOMA was able to carefully craft the negative usable space with incredible flexibility. This mass was conceived as larger than the existing walls, only to be sliced by a new glass storefront, effectively engaging the "fourth wall" of the sidewalk. This mass, created with a parametric script, manifests itself as a series of uniform white twenty-by-twenty-inch cubes. The result is a space that is quite literally sculpted by light.

The basement provides a more intimate setting in which products are displayed, the various light fixtures in a series of niches along narrow corridors. The walls and floor are rendered in a highly reflective black, while the niches are white, highlighting the individual characteristics of each fixture displayed.

Status
Built

Year
2013

Firm
SOMA

Firm location
New York, NY, USA

Awards Category **Typology & Plus** / Type **Commercial: Pop-Ups & Temporary, Architecture + Self Initiated Projects** / Winner **Jury & Popular Choice**

Boombox Micro Retail Chicago, IL, USA

Boombox Micro Retail is a prefabricated retail kiosk made from a refurbished shipping container and reinterpreted material qualities, introducing new ways for micro structure to intervene in Chicago's urban public spaces.

Boombox Micro Retail, located in Chicago and designed by Chicago-based firm Latent Design, is a prefabricated microretail kiosk made from a refurbished shipping container. Boombox is available for a wide variety of uses from selling clothing to launching a microbrew. It combines the successful features of pop-up shops and festival booths while providing innovative transitional retail spaces at competitive weekly rates.

The design of Boombox strips the container aesthetic away and replaces it with a "supercorrugation" large enough to fit ample adjustable shelves for product display outside the narrow footprint of the container. The modular exterior corrugation fins are clad on the interior with whitewashed plywood and the exterior with Hardie Board. A large accordion door allows the structure to instantly transform from a fully conditioned storefront to performance stage.

While "cargo-tecture" has been prominent for years across the globe, development of this type of architecture was nascent in Chicago. In order to create the first Boombox, Latent Design wrote new municipal policy that has fundamentally changed how public space, microstructures, and social enterprises can exist within the city of Chicago.

Status
Built

Year
2015

Firm
Latent Design

Firm location
Chicago, IL, USA

Awards Category Typology / Type Commercial: Pop-Ups & Temporary / Winner Popular Choice

The ANTI-KIOSK Quito, Ecuador

The exterior skin of the ANTI-KIOSK is hand-woven from traditional totora, and can adapt to showcase the nature of the client´s work, challenging preconceived ideas of the mall kiosk.

The ANTI-KIOSK revolutionizes the concept of the commercial island and transforms the shopping experience.

Inspired by rounded puzzles from the architect´s childhood, this six piece modular structure opens and closes, allowing for versatility and flexibility of arrangements depending on contextual conditions. The six wedges can be organized into endless configurations, forming various environments within one space. All of the pieces fit together, including a sales counter, storage compartments, display stands, as well as all of the products on display. Standing at 3.2 meters high, the ANTI-KIOSK can adapt to or be tailored to any product or service, showcasing the nature of the client´s work.

The exterior skin of the structure is made from traditional totora, a plant used as a building material by the South American Pre-Inca people, and is hand-woven by local artisans from Ecuador. Wallpaper designed by the client is displayed on the interior surfaces, as one of their many products. The sobriety of the exterior totora skin contrasting with the vivid wallpaper creates a dynamic spatial experience both inside and outside of the structure, breaking spatial boundaries.

The ANTI-KIOSK challenges every preconceived idea of what a mall kiosk should be, transporting its users outside of the mall context.

Status
Built

Year
2015

Firm
odD+

Firm location
Quito, Ecuador

Awards Category **Typology** / Type **Commercial: Office Interiors** / Winner **Jury**

Black Ocean Firehouse New York, NY, USA

Black Ocean Firehouse is a five-story building that was renovated into an incubator for small tech start-ups, juxtaposing wood paneling with graphic fluorescent lighting to create an energetic creative environment.

This converted firehouse, originally built in 1895, serves as an incubator for small tech start-ups. The five-story space houses offices of variable sizes from executive pods to four-person private offices to sixteen-person open offices. These multiple scenarios support a diverse range of start-up teams and allow for flexible groupings as companies come and go.

Unprescribed spaces such as stadium lounge seating, a roof terrace, and a back courtyard allow for larger presentations, informal meetings, and leisure, which promotes communal interaction. Wood paneling is juxtaposed with graphic fluorescent lighting to create a refined but energetic and creative environment.

Status
Built

Year
2013

Firm
Rafael de Cárdenas

Firm location
New York, NY, USA

Awards Category Typology / Type **Commercial: Office Interiors** / Winner **Popular Choice**

Flamingo Shanghai Office — The Attic Shanghai, China

Neri & Hu renovates an industrial roof space in Shanghai into offices by adding a steel A-frame structure to a flat roof so that the design enhances the experience of the existing roof conditions.

In Gaston Bachelard's work *The Poetics of Space* he suggests a metaphor of the house as a dwelling for the psyche. While the subterranean cellar represents our deep subconscious, the elevated attic is a space of quiet and rational thought. Neri & Hu's renovation of an industrial roof space in Shanghai into offices for a leading consulting firm is inspired by these very enigmatic notions of the attic.

Essentially a flat roof converted to occupied space with the addition of a steel A-frame structure, the design aims to exaggerate and enhance the experience of the existing roof conditions. The insertion of house-like volumes into a landscape of concrete platforms breaks down the homogenous space, such that the roof is not just a singular element but can be experienced on multiple levels.

Traversing the open work area, one first experiences an extensive view of the original structures, while black metal mesh panels frame bright clerestory windows above. The exhibition area features a pure floating roof to encapsulate the space while leaving it open and flexible. The board room, on the other hand, is completely enclosed, but also captures the double pitched roof and features lighting fixtures that mimic natural skylights.

Status
Built

Year
2014

Firm
Neri & Hu

Firm location
Shanghai, China

Awards Category Typology / Type Commercial: Factory Warehouse / Winner Jury & Popular Choice

Valdemonjas Winery Valladolid, Spain

Captivated by the local landscape and its topography, Agag+Paredes designed the Valdemonjas Winery to optimise the passive and sustainable resources used in winemaking.

Valdemonjas Winery is a family-owned winemaking business in the Ribera de Duero, Spain. The architects were captivated at first sight with the landscape.

The winery is oriented on an east-west axis. It sits on the topography, allowing the grape to enter the building by gravity. The main activities of winemaking happen at basement level: a central flexible space for fermentation, barrel washing, bottling, and labeling. The Barrel Hall is conceived as a breathable brick vaulted space. It benefits from the underground conditions of temperature and humidity.

The building's orientation, volume, facade, natural ventilation, and internal layout are designed to maximize passive sustainable resources. The building is not connected to the electric grid or to the main water system. The roof inclines to collect rainwater, which is stored for a year's use, and photovoltaic panels are integrated in the Entrance Canopy roof.

The client needed a strong image for the winery, leading the architects to design the building as a compact concrete volume emerging from the fields in a sea of vineyards.

The wine tasting area focuses on the pleasures of wine degustation, with natural light, amazing views, and a direct connection to the Barrel Hall and Cellar underground.

Status
Built

Year
2015

Firm
Agag+Paredes

Firm location
Madrid, Spain

Awards Category **Typology** / Type **Commercial: Mixed Use** / Winner **Jury & Popular Choice**

House of Vans London London, UK

The House of Vans London is a new mixed-use creative venue for skateboarding enthusiasts, composed of five separate tunnels, three of which are dedicated to a skatepark.

The House of Vans London is the recently completed project by Tim Greatrex Architect together with Hellicar&Lewis.

The project is a new mixed-use creative venue for Vans enthusiasts and those interested in skateboarding culture, established as a place to participate in the cultural lineage of skateboarding that has defined the Vans brand since 1966, combining skateboarding, art, film, and music. The new venue includes an art gallery, "Vans labs" creative spaces, a screening room, a music venue for 850 people, a premium café, numerous bars, and a three-tier indoor concrete skate park.

The site is delineated into these four main functions, each housed within a specific tunnel. The main function is the skatepark which accommodates three tunnel spaces to allow for varying layouts and abilities. The main space is the concrete "bowl" predominantly for advanced or professional use; the second area is the "street scene" for medium ability, and the third is the "mini ramp" skate park area for beginners or relaxed users.

The five separate tunnels of the site are unified with the large and impressive rubber floor inspired by the iconic patterned sole of the Vans shoe, hexagons and diamonds.

Status
Built

Year
2014

Firm
Tim Greatrex Architect

Firm location
London, UK

Awards Category **Typology** / Type **Commercial: Unbuilt Commercial** / Winner **Popular Choice**

Reservoir Rajasthan, India

Sanjay Puri Architects imagines an office building amid dry desert land, where contours and landscaping address the difficulties of the site in making an ecologically conscious complex.

This site is located in Rajasthan amidst desert land where water is a scarcity and temperatures are in excess of 105 degrees Fahrenheit eight months of the year.

The site is steeply contoured, and the land forms a natural water collection pit. To capitalize on that water collection, stepped wells—built in Rajasthan for centuries—were studied. The design of the built form is directly inspired by those ancient wells.

Office spaces are created on the two north-facing sides, gradually stepping down at each level along the existing contours, generating north-facing landscaped terraces.

The opposite south-facing sides are shaped into open stepped platforms along the site's contours, further generating landscaped spaces and creating a large community space.

The southern side is protected by earth berms that rise to create sheltered parking spaces, with lower berms on the northern sides.

The design is responsive to the site contours, the climate of its location, and the needs of its users. It generates office spaces that require much lower energy consumption due to their orientation while reflecting the traditional architecture prevalent in the region and creating a large water catchment.

Status
Concept

Firm
Sanjay Puri Architects

Firm location
Mumbai, India

Awards Category Typology / Type **Hospitality: Hotels & Resorts** / Winner **Jury**

Sandibe Safari Lodge Okovango Delta, Botswana

The sustainably-built and alimented Sandibe Safari Lodge foregrounds a dramatic timber design and twelve elevated suites that sit in a forest canopy, looking over the shimmering delta.

Sandibe Safari Lodge is a sustainable new-build safari lodge located on a UNESCO World Heritage Site in northwest Botswana. The brief was to replace the previous lodge with a dramatic design, providing a lighter, more sustainable footprint while capturing the tranquility of the Okavango Delta region.

The lodge consists of a dramatic timber main building and twelve elevated private bedroom suites that sit within a forest canopy of wild palms and fig trees. Each building is positioned for unrestricted views of the shimmering delta.

On arrival, guests walk through a bower woven from saplings and laths. Curved steps lead through segments of shingled skin to the entrance of the main building and a raised dining terrace. A half flight of stairs ascends to the lounge area with a dramatic curved bar and sweeping timber ribs.

Sandibe was successfully designed with a sustainable approach, with all concrete removed, none used in new construction, and 70 percent of energy consumption provided from renewable energy sources.

The structures are clad in cedar shingles and constructed with treated glulam South African pine beams and eucalyptus gum poles sourced from sustainable forests.

Status
Built

Year
2014

Firm
Michaelis Boyd

Firm location
London, UK

Awards Category Typology / Type Hospitality: Restaurants / Winner Jury

Mirrors Gifu City, Gifu Prefecture, Japan

This Japanese roadside café takes the archetypal house form and slices it open to reveal mirrored stainless steel facades that infinitely reflect a single blossom into a forest of trees.

Mirrors is a roadside café designed for a plot by a row of cherry trees. Taking advantage of this location, Mirrors reflects the cherry blossom, creating a forest and inviting visitors inside. The building has two wings and looks as if it has been split in half symmetrically and arranged around a single camellia tree, which stands on a patch of white gravel with tile edging. The cherry blossoms are mirrored by the reflective gables.

The reflective gables are made of stainless steel and the reflection's distorted image creates unusual scenery. In the gables, the visitors notice the trees both directly and indirectly via reflection. Simultaneously, the unexpected occurrences make the visitors not only enjoy the cherry blossom but also feel the sensitive transition of four seasons through green foliage, fallen leaves, and the camellia that blooms when the weather turns.

Status
Built

Year
2014

Firm
bandesign

Firm location
Nagoya City, Japan

Awards Category **Typology** / Type **Hospitality: Restaurants** / Winner **Popular Choice**

Forestaurant Hanoi, Vietnam

H&P Architects' Forestaurant is a space that recalls ancient trees, while the entire existing steel structure is welded to conceal a new system of technical pipes inside the restaurant.

Located in the center of Hanoi, Forestaurant is a renovation of a long-closed project and still retains its steel-frame structure and some reusable covering materials such as glass, steel, bar steel, and sheet-metal roofing.

The designers created a space that recalls ancient trees, which are a familiar image in the streets of this 1,000-year-old city.

Their solution proposed welding the existing steel to create a new system that could bring technical pipes inside, covered by wood bars forming larger timbers of fifteen inches by fifteen inches.

The timbers stack perpendicularly to each other and gradually spread upwards in order to create "tree roots" for separating spaces and creating a children's playground. The tree roots continue growing to make a stable frame that helps reduce heat and create various shadows from the polycarbonate roof. In the middle of the roof is an air layer, cooled and cleaned automatically by a water spraying system linked to a rainwater collection tank.

The project creates special experiences for the user and brings people closer to nature through a space that contains the essence of the iconic Hanoi sidewalk culture.

Status
Built

Year
2014

Firm
H&P Architects

Firm location
Hanoi, Vietnam

Awards Category Typology / Type Hospitality: Bars & Nightclubs / Winner Jury

Charles Smith Wines Jet City Seattle, WA, USA

After various lives as an industrial plant, the new Charles Smith Wines Jet City serves for both the production and enjoyment of its products, and connects with the street through a nineteen-by-sixty-foot window.

Originally constructed to house a Dr. Pepper bottling plant and later a recycling center, the new Charles Smith Wines Jet City preserves much of the building's hard-won industrial patina, while opening up the facade to the surrounding Georgetown neighborhood, Boeing Field, and Mt. Rainier.

The former 32,000-square-foot building is composed of two structures: a two-floor office building and an open-structure, steel truss warehouse. Together, they provide space for grape crushing, barrel storage, and bottling to tasting rooms and sales space. The transformation of this 1960s-era building involved the removal of a portion of the exterior street-side facade, replacing it with a span of nineteen-foot-by-sixty-foot windows.

Once through the twenty-foot-tall steel entry door, visitors have the choice of two tasting rooms. The rustic, entry-level lounge features polished concrete floors, exposed wood joists, sliding black steel wall panels, and a bar made of stacked, salvaged wood.

A plate-steel staircase inserted into the original structure connects the first-floor lounge to the expansive second-floor tasting room. The winery's second story effectively captures an early 1960s aviation vibe with its original wood floor planks, white tuck-and-roll upholstered perimeter seating, and center stage powder-blue, Lucite-topped bar on wheels.

Status
Built

Year
2015

Firm
Olson Kundig

Firm location
Seattle, WA, USA

Awards Category Typology / Type **Hospitality: Bars & Nightclubs** / Winner **Popular Choice**

Odin Bar + Café Toronto, ON, Canada

Privileging natural light and integrated bar furniture, Odin Bar + Café is an inviting setting for the new culture of workers.

A café/bar hybrid, Odin embraces its neighborhood's newly refined industrial aesthetic, along with the changing culture of how people work and socialize, and the playful complexity that comes with a day-to-night transformation. Columns divide the space, naturally defining the front-of-house area between a high-traffic bar and relaxed, low-table seating. Bar-height seating at the column line replicates the mass of the columns at a human scale. Corian and plywood panels over plywood ribs transform to unify the numerous café elements. The result is a singular form that transitions between monolithic sculpture and its skeletal framework, ultimately simplifying the design while maintaining a dynamic and nuanced expression of the various performing parts.

Bar equipment is fully cloaked behind a solid object that is heavy and grounded against the concrete floor. This seemingly monolithic object transforms, revealing itself as panels over the structure that provides its form. This exposed structure serves as shelving with integrated retail, sound equipment, and overhead storage. As the ceiling moves away from the bar, it breaks apart to create a directional pattern that draws the eye out towards the street during the day and in from the street at night.

Status
Built

Year
2015

Firm
Phaedrus Studio

Firm location
Toronto, ON, Canada

Awards Category Typology / Type Hospitality: Health Care & Wellness / Winner Jury & Popular Choice

Naman Retreat Pure Spa Da Nang City, Vietnam

Lush open-air gardens of local plants, deep-soak bathtubs, and cushioned daybeds make the setting for this naturally-ventilated and luxurious spa.

The Naman Retreat Pure Spa is an oasis of tranquility. Fifteen stunning treatment rooms are endowed with lush open-air gardens, deep-soak bathtubs, and cushioned daybeds built for two. Visitors can keep fit at the equally sleek health club with gym, meditation, and yoga sessions held in the open lounge garden. The ground floor contains open spaces with relaxing platforms surrounded by serene lotus ponds and hanging gardens.

MIA Design Studio's ingenious use of natural ventilation keeps the building cool and gives the guest a refreshing experience. With the use of local plants, each retreat becomes a healing environment where the guest can enjoy luxurious wellness in privacy.

Different areas flow smoothly into each other, and the beautiful landscape creates an amazing journey into a dreamlike experience. The facade is composed of lattice patterns alternated with vertical gardens that filter the strong tropical sunlight into a pleasant play of light and shadow on the textured walls. Various plants, carefully allocated, become a part of the architectural screens.

Status
Built

Year
2015

Firm
MIA Design Studio

Firm location
Ho Chi Minh City, Vietnam

Awards Category Typology / Type Hospitality: Unbuilt Hospitality / Winner Jury

Destination Spa + Resort

Bordering desert and sea, Destination Spa + Resort merges with its wondrous environment, as its gardens, pools, and meditative areas imagine a romantic setting influenced by local culture.

In an ethereal landscape at the edge of the desert and sea, this new resort and spa is framed within the founding principles of one of the most timeless and influential civilizations. It is intensity without spectacle, singular not only in the clarity of the composition, but also in the quiet power of each component. The monumental architecture of the past celebrated the dead and the heavens above; this architecture celebrates the wonderful possibilities of life on this earth.

Destination Spa + Resort merges silently with its wondrous setting, seamlessly integrated with the earth. Here the topographic transition from the desert dunescapes to the beach creates a welcome transition from the sand to the sea. It stays true to the ancient vernacular traditions of in-earth building, having a reverence for the landscape and the materials of the region. The nature of the discrete and selective carvings in the earth provides several opportunities for drama and surprise. Gardens, pools, and meeting and meditative areas are all found in the interstitial spaces.

Status
Concept

Firm
Oppenheim Architecture

Firm location
Miami, FL, USA

Awards Category Typology / Type Hospitality: Unbuilt Hospitality / Winner Popular Choice

Centre Hospitalier de l'Université de Montréal Montréal, QC, Canada

Through quality in massing, composition, material strategies, clearly defined exterior and interior public spaces, and art and heritage integration, this hospital was envisioned to act not only as a place of healing but as a place of gathering.

Hospitals are for the public: the users that inhabit the building on a daily, weekly, or monthly basis, and the broader community that holds its own well-being in high regard. Through its design and creation, the CHUM (Centre Hospitalier de l'Université de Montreal) was envisioned to act not only as a place of healing, but as a place of gathering.

The hospital's patients, employees, and professionals required the integration of three existing and outdated healthcare facilities into one massive patient-led healthcare facility, the largest new hospital in North America. It will contain a center for research and a teaching hospital for students and residents, all while preserving and promoting a culture of care and well-being.

Through quality in massing, composition, material strategies, clearly defined exterior and interior public spaces, art and heritage integration, and the very forefront of healthcare planning, the project carries a symbolic component of the healthcare system of Québec. A strategy of transparency ensures the building is constantly engaging the public, with animation within the building visible from the street and vice versa. Open spaces occur throughout the project in strategic locations, providing orientation, sunlight, contemplative spaces, and views to the city.

Status
Under Construction

Year
2020

Firm
CannonDesign and NEUF Architect(e)s

Firm location
Montréal, QC, Canada and Other Locations

Awards Category **Typology** / Type **Sport & Recreation: Stadium/Arena** / Winner **Jury**

Ocean Breeze Track and Field House Staten Island, NY, USA

The solution to building a fieldhouse on a delicate environmental site was to minimize the footprint by elevating it to locate a parking space below, and to allow bandwidth for incorporating photovoltaic technology on the roof.

As part of New York City's initiative for design excellence, and with the Department of Parks and Recreation, Sage and Coombe Architects were selected to design the 135,000-square-foot track and fieldhouse in the new 110-acre Ocean Breeze Park.

The building is slated for one of the few remaining areas of native upland coastal grasslands on the island. The solution was to minimize the footprint by raising the building and locating required parking below, enhancing both views and the potential for natural ventilation.

The approach to the building starts with an inclined walk that brings the visitor and the athlete to a terrace overlooking the expansive parkland beyond. The project integrates green building principles in water management, daylighting, and natural ventilation, with the potential for future incorporation of photovoltaic technology on the roof.

The fieldhouse will include a 200-meter hydraulically banked track meeting USATF, NCAA, and IAFF competition standards; seating for 2,500; a fitness center, café, and concessions; and restrooms and service spaces. Concealed beneath the building are 140 naturally ventilated parking spaces.

The project is seeking LEED Silver Certification and has been honored with a 2009 Design Award from the NYC Design Commission.

Status
Under Construction

Year
2015

Firm
Sage and Coombe Architects

Firm location
New York, NY, USA

Awards Category Typology / Type **Sport & Recreation: Stadium/Arena** / Winner **Popular Choice**

Rovaniemi Sports Arena Rovaniemi, Finland

The central sports arena designed by APRT forms a reindeer's eye in Alvar Aalto's design of the reindeer horn city plan, which was drawn as part of grand efforts to reconstruct Rovaniemi after World War Two.

A new multi-purpose building was completed in Rovaniemi in July. It houses a stadium for 2,000 people as well as athletic changing rooms and washrooms. The project is an essential part of a central sports arena in the city center of Rovaniemi.

The city of Rovaniemi was destroyed in World War II. As a basis for its reconstruction, architect Alvar Aalto designed the reindeer horn city plan for Rovaniemi in 1946. The central sports arena forms the reindeer's eye in that plan. The arena has become the townspeople's recreational venue for activities including track, field, and football.

The main trusses of steel and plywood form a zigzag facade towards the northeast. Rising sixty feet from the surface of the arena, those trusses form a powerful visual motif, changing depending on the lighting and visual angle.

Seen from the arena, the graded stand with a concrete structure creates a landscape dotted with colorful seats and wind nets.

Status
Built

Year
2015

Firm
APRT (Arkkitehtityöhuone Artto Palo Rossi Tikka Architects)

Firm location
Helsinki, Finland

Awards Category Typology / Type Sport & Recreation: Recreation Centers / Winner Jury

Nathalie Mauclair Gymnasium Champagné, Sarthe, France

A glulam structure coated with a metal cladding and woven around translucent polycarbonate facades gives the Nathalie Mauclair Gymnasium a visually dynamic volume.

In 2013, the town of Champagné launched a consultation on building a multi-sport hall to offer a wider range of sports activities, and to relieve pressure on the Jean Rondeau gymnasium. The city wanted the new sports hall and the existing gymnasium to be joined together.

A coherent whole is obtained with continuity in height and a refined connection between the existing gymnasium and the multi-sport hall.

The crystalline hall space emerges from a low register that integrates the second building and aligns at the high level of the galleries of the existing gymnasium. The roof of this link is made accessible, and functions as an external meeting place common to both buildings.

A glulam structure coated with a metal cladding is woven around the translucent polycarbonate box that makes up the volume of the hall.

Polycarbonate facades, with their reflective character, allow the building to evolve constantly. Changes in light during the day generate changing colors, moving reflections, and a dynamic character.

The north side, being very open, allows one to enjoy a diffuse light throughout the day. At the south facade, the base is made opaque to avoid glare problems for players.

Status
Built

Year
2015

Firm
SCHEMAA

Firm location
Paris, France

Awards Category Typology / Type Sport & Recreation: Recreation Centers / Winner Popular Choice

Sohanak Swimming Pool Tehran, Iran

In a private garden in Tehran, the Sohanak Swimming Pool transforms an existing irrigation pool into an outdoor swimming pool, and builds in a kiosk, a typical landmark in traditional Iranian gardens.

Located in a private garden in the northwest side of Tehran, this swimming pool project sits on a flat area atop a small hill with views of the surrounding gardens and the city.

Kourosh Rafiey decided to transform the existing irrigation pool into an outdoor swimming pool with adequate space for a sauna, a Jacuzzi, and other related spaces such as lockers, showers, washrooms, and a spacious deck for sunbathing and diving.

Since this building is exactly on the main axes of the garden, the architects designed it as a kiosk, a traditional Iranian garden structure. The parameters distinguished by four facades, a void in the main facade, and a reflection of the building image on the water's surface.

The other issue was to develop a mutual interaction between architecture and landscape. Therefore, the whole building is wrapped in a continuous surface, connected to the pool from one side and a green area from the other side. The subsequent gap is filled with water, creating a unique illusion in the process. The structure is completed by a spacious deck overlooking the pool.

Status
Built

Year
2014

Firm
Kourosh Rafiey Architectural Design Studio (KRDS)

Firm location
Tehran, Iran

Awards Category **Typology** / Type **Sport & Recreation: Unbuilt Sport & Recreation** / Winner **Jury & Popular Choice**

Polur Rock Gym Polur, Iran

The Polur Rock Climbing Hall is a proposal inspired by the geological process of large-scale movements of the earth's crust and its tectonic forces.

The project site is a part of the Mount Damavand region located north of Tehran, Iran. Mount Damavand is a significant mountain in Persian mythology and has a special place in Persian literature.

For the first challenge, there were key parameters to achieve an intimate identity with the natural surroundings. Overall, the architects were looking for something new and a dialogue between artifice and nature. As such, Polur Rock Climbing Hall is inspired by the geological process of large-scale movements of the earth's crust and its tectonic forces.

This is a project where concept is form, context is nature, and content is function, with all of these three factors interacting with each other. The architecture strives to be generous, demanding, memorable, interactive, and sustainable.

Visually, the building appears to push itself out of the layers of the earth's crust, stemming from the land. The project rises, peaks, and gradually moves down its mountainous backdrop.

Status
Under Construction

Year
2018

Firm
New Wave Architecture

Firm location
Tehran, Iran

Awards Category Typology / Type Cultural: Unbuilt Cultural / Winner Jury & Popular Choice

Anti-Museum Toronto, ON, Canada

Aiming to redesign the southern set of silos in Toronto's Harbourfront area, Diamond Schmitt Architects has conceived an Anti-Museum that stems from the Romantics' admiration of ancient ruins.

Romantic artists and intellectuals of the nineteenth century were awed by the grandeur and sublimity of ancient ruins that mingled the natural and the man-made in a unique time and space. That reciprocal consummation of nature and architecture sits in contrast with the idealized image of building as everlasting monument, frozen in a pristine state.

The project takes these ideas of nature and seeks to reintroduce them to the architecture of the present time. The wilderness of the nineteenth century is long since gone in today's urban environments and has evolved into a broader and more diverse existence, internalized by modern society.

As a significant part of Toronto's Harbourfront area, this site offers challenges and opportunities. The project aligns itself with (and is a part of) the ongoing Bathurst Quay Neighborhood Development Plan. It focuses on redesigning the southern set of these silos, inside a larger redevelopment proposal for the entire property and vicinity. It includes a museum, an extension to the Harbourfront Community Centre, and site developments to address accessibility issues for the promenade, the Ireland Park, and the Billy Bishop airport.

Status
Concept

Firm
Diamond Schmitt Architects/Siavash Vazirnezami, Intern Architect

Firm location
Toronto, ON, Canada

Awards Category **Typology & Plus** / Type **Cultural: Museum, Architecture + Landscape** / Winner **Jury & Popular Choice**

Biesbosch MuseumEiland Werkendam, The Netherlands

The Biesbosch MuseumEiland is the starting point for visitors exploring the Biesbosch National Park, hence the necessity to conceive and execute this expansion in an ecological and sustainable way.

After an eight-month renovation, the Biesbosch MuseumEiland has reopened to the public. The museum has been completely transformed and extended with a new wing that opens to its beautiful surroundings and houses a restaurant and temporary exhibition space for contemporary art. The permanent exhibition on the historical development of the region has also been totally revamped. A large water model of the Biesbosch and a freshwater tidal park are also planned.

Building, interior, water model, and freshwater tidal park were designed by Studio Marco Vermeulen. The exhibition was designed by Studio Joyce Langezaal.

Water safety was the key reason for the development of the Biesbosch MuseumEiland. As part of a national water safety program, the location has been turned into a water-retention area. Outlets on either side of the Biesbosch MuseumEiland were dug to create a new island.

The hexagonal structure of the original Biesbosch MuseumEiland pavilions has been retained, and a new 10,764-square-foot wing was added on the southwestern side of the building. With extensive windows, the wing opens to the museum garden on the island.

Status
Built

Year
2015

Firm
Studio Marco Vermeulen

Firm location
Rotterdam, The Netherlands

Awards Category Typology / Type Cultural: Museum / Winner Popular Choice
Messner Mountain Museum Corones Kronplatz, South Tyrol, Italy

Established by renowned climber Reinhold Messner, the Messner Mountain Museum explores the traditions, history, and discipline of mountaineering, while its form reflects the impressive landscape of the Italian Alps.

Embedded within the summit of Mount Kronplatz, 7,460 feet above sea level at the center of South Tyrol's most popular ski resort, the Messner Mountain Museum Corones is surrounded by the alpine peaks of the Zillertal, Ortler, and Dolomites. Established by renowned climber Reinhold Messner, the sixth and final iteration of the Messner Mountain Museum explores the traditions, history, and discipline of mountaineering.

The museum welcomes visitors throughout the year to explore Messner's world, where humanity is pushed to its limits, adding a further cultural and educational institution to Mount Kronplatz.

Informed by the shards of rock and ice of the surrounding landscape, concrete canopies have been cast in situ and rise from the ground to protect the museum's entrance, viewing windows, and terrace. Reflecting the lighter colors and tones of the jagged limestone peaks of the surrounding Dolomites, the exterior panels are formed from a lighter shade of glass-reinforced fiber concrete, and fold within the museum to meet the darker interior panels that have the coloration of anthracite. A series of staircases, like waterfalls in a mountain stream, cascade through the museum to connect the exhibition spaces.

Status
Built

Year
2015

Firm
Zaha Hadid Architects

Firm location
London, UK

Awards Category **Typology** / Type **Cultural: Gallery** / Winner **Jury**
National Design Centre Singapore

In concert with an existing structure, the National Design Centre reinvents its contribution to the district of Bras Basah in Singapore with efforts to activate the street frontage with interactive public areas.

This insertion into the National Design Centre is a showcase of innovation. It forms a unique contribution to the urban fabric in the conservation district of Bras Basah, regenerating an existing structure to form a varied, flexible space for interaction and learning.

Conceptually, the design is a composition of four translucent boxes constructed in steel frames and aluminum mesh screens, cantilevering and overlapping to form an interconnected series of volumes for both public and private use.

The design respects the existing building with an insertion that serves to enhance the spaces within. To promote open courtyard interaction, the aluminum-clad boxes operate as a new feature within the central space, and provide areas for exhibitions. These boxes are detached from the external facade, creating a three-story interstitial volume that filters light down to the gallery.

The proposal also addresses the need to activate the street frontage by arranging key public areas on the first level. A bistro café links the street to the central courtyard and flows into a space for retail and exhibition.

Status
Built

Year
2013

Firm
SCDA Architects
Singapore

Firm location
Singapore

Awards Category **Typology** / Type **Cultural: Gallery** / Winner **Popular Choice**

CTAA Architecture Lab Tainan, Taiwan

The baseball diamond located in this gallery is designed to make Taiwan's favorite sport accessible to Taiwan's children, creating a bridge between play and the spirit of innovation and possibility.

In the historic center of Tainan city sits a unique modern creation. Overlooking narrow streets filled with lively crowds and traditional temples, its design bursts forth from Taiwan's traditional landscape like a white lotus.

The internal structure of the core office space is divided into three different spaces to encourage individual innovation while maintaining a cohesive sharing unit.

The most unusual feature is the baseball diamond, designed to make Taiwan's favorite sport accessible to Taiwan's children. Due to a lack of space, equipment, and economic means, playing baseball is not a possibility for many of Tainan's children. This state-of-the-art building, creates a bridge between Taiwan's one hundred-year-old beloved sport, traditional culture, and the spirit of innovation and possibility.

Status
Built

Year
2015

Firm
CTAA Architect Lab

Firm location
Tainan, Taiwan

Awards Category **Typology** / Type **Cultural: Hall/Theater** / Winner **Jury**
The Shakespearean Theatre Gdansk, Poland

In addition to its intricate brick aesthetic, the Shakespearean Theatre offers three ways to stage performances: with an open roof, in a traditional setting, and in an arena layout.

It has taken almost a quarter century to become a reality, but the Gdansk Shakespearean Theatre is now open to the public. Located next to the remnants of the city's fourteenth-century walls, the exterior contains some of the Gothic elements that dominate the style of Gdansk's Old Town.

The facades feature hand-formed anthracite brick. Gdansk has a predominantly red-brick aesthetic, and the architects were inspired by the nearby medieval churches to introduce a dark material contrast.

There are three ways to stage a performance: with an open roof (the Elizabethan style), in a traditional setting (the audience is in front of the stage), and in an arena layout (the scene is surrounded by the audience). The narrow corridors around the audience seating lead to a large lobby and an outdoor patio. This is where the audience can congregate during intermission. The outdoor roof terraces also provide an attractive view, allowing visitors to see the city from a different perspective.

Beams appear in the outer walls. These beams absorb the load from the sunroof and reduce the weight of the walls, allowing for structural optimization. The high wall hides the theatre's mechanisms and technical equipment.

Status
Built

Year
2015

Firm
Vandersanden Group

Firm location
Bilzen, Belgium

Awards Category **Typology** / Type **Cultural: Hall / Theater** / Winner **Popular Choice**

Great Amber — Concert Hall Liepaja, Latvia

This cone-shaped, slightly contorted concrete structure with a transparent, amber-colored facade envelops the building's most important architectural element: a 1,000-seat concert hall

The Great Amber is a monolithic, cone-shaped, slightly tilted structure with a transparent, amber-colored facade. This facade envelops the irregular folded work of the concrete structure built around the building's most important architectural element: the 1,000-seat concert hall. The hall itself is surrounded by the facilities of the Liepaja Symphony Orchestra and the music school's instruction and rehearsal rooms, a favorable blend of spaces to foster communication between artists, students, and teachers. An additional chamber hall situated beneath the concert hall, a ballet studio, an experimental stage, and a bar and music club on the fifth floor complete the spatial concept.

The acoustics were based on the principle of an oval, terraced vineyard. Reaching high above the roof, fourteen mirror-finished reflective tubes flood the concert hall with daylight, creating a unique atmosphere inside.

Attached to a delicately interwoven steel construction, the amber-colored glazing bathes the inside in soft warm light. At night the building turns into a transparent luminous element, making its interior and many functions visible from the outside. During the day, the building's external glazing glows in varying colors and shades.

Status
Built

Year
2015

Firm
Volker Giencke & Company

Firm location
Graz, Austria

Awards Category Typology / Type **Cultural: Religious Buildings & Memorials** / Winner **Jury**

Crematorium Hofheide Holsbeek, Belgium

The Crematorium Hofheide, set in the Flemish plain's vast landscape, subtly accomodates spaces for gathering and consolation, while the more functional aspects of the building are set at a different level out of respect for the mourners.

The Flemish plain is a vast landscape that shapes a gentle, swampy basin at this site. This basin is the setting for the crematorium, as well as the larger reservoir, which is part of a walk through the park that spreads across the entire precinct, at the opposite ends of which are two cemeteries (one for burials, the other for niches).

    The Crematorium Hofheide subtly accommodates the actions of mourning, including gathering together for consolation in a space that is as close to nature as possible, enhancing one's sense that one is a part of it. Another important conceit of the project is its readiness for nondenominational leave-taking ceremonies in a space that provides shelter for grief, music, embraces, and words. The more functional aspects are set at a different level of the pavilion so as not to hinder the outpouring of these sentiments.

Status
Built

Year
2014

Firm
RCR Arquitectes

Firm location
Olot, Spain

Awards Category Typology / Type Cultural: Religious Buildings & Memorials / Winner Popular Choice

Sayama Forest Chapel Tokorozawa City, Saitama, Japan

On a small triangular plot of land, Hiroshi Nakamura & NAP creates a space devoted to the forest, a traditional Japanese Gassho-style structure adapted to the nature-rich environment.

Sayama Lakeside Cemetery is open to various religions and denominations. It is located in a nature-rich environment adjacent to a water conservation area, and in front of a deep forest. Its creators envisioned an architecture that reflects on life as it lives by the water conserved by the forest, and eventually returns to this place after death.

The site is a small triangular plot of land adjacent to a municipal road, a low traffic street with almost no pedestrians. The architects decided to create a space devoted to the forest by tilting the wall inward to avoid tree branches and leaves. It forms a traditional Japanese Gassho-style structure composed three-dimensionally as two leaning beams set against each other, and developed in every direction. The roof is covered in cast-aluminum tiles with ripple-like textures, each made by local craftsmen.

The floor, inclined towards the forest by two inches, guides people towards the departed and the forward-bending posture for praying. The patterns and seams of the slate extend towards a vanishing point deep in the forest, helping concentrate the mind on nature.

Status
Built

Year
2013

Firm
Hiroshi Nakamura & NAP

Firm location
Setagaya, Japan

Awards Category **Typology** / Type **Cultural: Pavilions** / Winner **Jury & Popular Choice**

UK Pavilion — Milan Expo 2015 Milan, Italy

The aim of the UK Pavilion is to highlight the plight of the honeybee, so the design integrates a network of 1,000 LED lights that react to real-time signals of vibrations experienced among a bee colony.

Artist Wolfgang Buttress led a multi-disciplinary team to create the UK Pavilion at the 2015 Expo in Milan, the theme of which was "Feeding the Planet Energy for Life."

The Pavilion has since been installed at Kew Gardens in England. Buttress' aim of the UK Pavilion was to highlight the plight of the honeybee and ways new research and technology are helping to address challenges such as food security and biodiversity. Visitors map the journey of the bee: meandering through an orchard, discovering a meadow of wild flowers, and entering the sculptural hive.

The Hive is an abstracted analogue of a honeycomb. A rotational twist in the structure introduces movement, suggestive of a swarm. The form is a forty-six-foot cube raised up on columns, appearing almost to hover above the meadow. A spherical void hollowed from the center allows visitors to enter.

Accelerometers (vibration sensors) are used to measure the activity of a real bee colony in the UK, feeding real-time signals to a 1,000 RGBW LED light array inside the spherical void. Algorithms are used to convert the bee colony vibrations into lighting effects. Each light is individually addressable, allowing for the Hive to pulse and glow in response to the signals it receives.

Status
Built

Year
2015

Firm
Wolfgang Buttress

Firm location
Nottingham, UK

Awards Category **Typology** / Type **Institutional: Government & Municipal Buildings** / Winner **Jury**

Expansion of Government Offices Alicante, Spain

Covered in a mosaic of enameled ceramic tiles, the eye-catching skin of this expansion of Alicante government offices hides the circular organization of its interior.

The unique feature of this project is its eye-catching facade, where ceramic tile is once again the protagonist. The facade represents the town council and attracts the citizens' attention: It forms a continuous covering that wraps around the whole uneven structure, covering vertical and horizontal surfaces with a mosaic of hexagonal tiles made of enameled ceramic.

The scale of the exterior may give the impression of a small, picturesque place. The interior of the pavilion is far from that. Access to the concrete structure is through one of the arms, a kind of vestibule, which leads to an extensive space that, thanks to its irregular shape, allows for several different areas in each of its corners.

The structure consists of a one-floor building formed by a series of trapezoids arranged in an irregular shape, almost a star, connected through a large central space. The layout of the trapezoids allows for a circular organization of the interior, so that the whole of the space can be seen from one point—the customer service desk—behind which there is a small office.

Status
Built

Year
2013

Firm
CrystalZoo

Firm location
Alicante, Spain

Awards Category Typology / Type **Institutional: Kindergartens** / Winner **Jury**

Hanazono Kindergarten and Nursery Okinawa, Japan

Designed by a Japanese architecture firm specializing in childcare architecture, Hanazono Kindergarten and Nursery draws from the traditional wooden, red-roof-tile architecture of subtropical Miyakojima to design a space where children's activity areas are all connected.

Hanazono Kindergarten and Nursery is located in Miyakojima, about 1,242 miles away from Tokyo. Miyakojima has a subtropical, oceanic climate and is surrounded by blue sea and coral reefs. The project was made to withstand typhoon conditions.

The building draws from the traditional wooden, red-roof-tile architecture seen in the area. The structure has a steel and reinforced concrete construction. Around the outer perimeter of the building low canopies and screens made by concrete blocks protect the school and shut out sunlight and wind. The color of the outer wall tile was chosen to match the traditional red-roof tile color of the region.

The studio shares a border with the playground, the atelier shares a border with the courtyard, and the dining area is surrounded by a terrace and courtyard. Children do sound play in the studio and do production activity in the atelier. The playground and dining garden have traditional plants and fruit-bearing trees.

Status
Built

Year
2015

Firm
HIBINOSEKKEI + Youji no Shiro

Firm location
Atsugi, Japan

Awards Category Typology / Type **Institutional: Kindergartens** / Winner **Popular Choice**

The Kindergarten of the German School of Athens Athens, Greece

This kindergarten design focuses on the experience the children will gain through cognitive and emotional interaction with the building and introduces a new geography at the scale of the complex.

The design for the Kindergarten of the German School of Athens is informed not merely by function but by the actions of the students. It endeavors to be a material semiotic system, a network of interactive relationships. This is an approach based on the stance that architectural space is not idle.

The architectural synthesis focuses on the experience that the children will gain through their cognitive and emotional correlation with the building. Thus, it introduces a new, small geography of the world. The design addresses the kindergarten as an object on a scale of 1:1. The volumes, shaped by white and wooden parts that constitute semi-open spaces, seek inspiration in the modules of a Lego-type system that, when added together, formulate the final composition.

The Kindergarten of the German School of Athens was nominated by the Mies Van der Rohe Foundation for the 2015 Mies Van der Rohe Awards.

Status
Built

Year
2014

Firm
Potiropoulos +Partners

Firm location
Athens, Greece

Awards Category **Typology** / Type **Institutional: Primary & High Schools** / Winner **Jury & Popular Choice**

P.S. 62 The Kathleen Grimm School for Leadership and Sustainability
Staten Island, NY, USA

One of the first net-zero energy school buildings in New York City, P.S. 62, the Kathleen Grimm School for Leadership and Sustainability, harvests its energy from renewable on-site resources.

P.S. 62, the Kathleen Grimm School for Leadership and Sustainability, is the first net-zero energy school in New York City and one of the first of its kind worldwide. The cutting-edge building achieves its net-zero energy target by harvesting energy from renewable on-site resources.

Located on the south shore of Staten Island, the 444-seat, 68,000-squarefoot primary school is designed to comply with the SCA Green Schools Guide developed specifically for New York City public schools. The client for the project was the New York City School Construction Authority on behalf of the New York City Department of Education.

Situated on three and a half acres, the school is oriented to the center of its L-shaped site in order to optimize natural light for photovoltaic panels and interior learning spaces. Thanks to its aggressive approach to sustainability, P.S. 62, the Kathleen Grimm School, achieves a remarkable 50 percent reduction in energy use over a typical new public school in New York.

The school's many sustainable design features include photovoltaic panels on the building's roofs and south facade, precast rain screens on three facades, skylights and reflective ceiling panels that amplify natural light, a geo-exchange heating and cooling system, energy recovery ventilators and demand-control ventilation, and a solar thermal system for hot water.

Status
Built

Year
2015

Firm
Skidmore, Owings & Merrill

Firm location
New York, NY, USA

Awards Category **Typology** / Type **Institutional: Higher Education & Research Facilities** / Winner **Jury**

Guessing Agriculture School Guessing, Austria

Laid out around a central courtyard, the lightweight timber architecture of the Guessing Agriculture School is topped with extensive green roofs, while the excavated earth sculpts the surrounding terrain.

The stables of the Guessing Agriculture School are laid out around a central courtyard. This ensures short routes and a clear overview from every point in the yard. A continuous canopy roof provides protection from the weather in accessing all parts of the complex. The stables are surrounded by open spaces, air, and sunlight. This establishes an adequate relationship to outdoor space for the animals.

In principle, three different tectonic levels are articulated, each of which is expressed by means of its respective materials: those parts that rest on the ground are made of concrete; the rising walls are built in a lightweight timber frame or timber rod construction; and the roofs are load-bearing wooden structures covered with extensive green planting.

The green roofs help buffer the impact of summer heat. The earth excavated in the course of the building work sculpts the surrounding terrain.

The stables extend like fingers into the surrounding landscape, and the complex looks more like a cluster than a traditional four-square farm or bastion. The buildings, consciously interpreted as part of the landscape, are folded out into the surrounding meadows.

Status
Built

Year
2015

Firm
Pichler & Traupmann Architekten

Firm location
Vienna, Austria

Awards Category Typology / Type Institutional: Higher Education & Research Facilities / Winner Popular Choice

School of Architecture — Royal Institute of Technology Stockholm, Sweden

Tham & Videgård Arkitekter's Corten-steel School of Architecture for the Royal Institute of Technology encases a robust and flexible program for students at this innovative college.

Based on the logic of a free campus layout that encourages movement, this design aims to accommodate and encourage circulation within the building and all around it as a way of thoroughly integrating the new school to the site. With its rounded contours and a total of six floors, the school building includes a sunken garden and a roof terrace, while cultivating the character of the courtyard as one continuous space. The deep red Corten-steel exterior relates to the dark red brick of existing buildings.

The interior is designed to be robust and flexible. Curving walls create a free flow of contiguous spaces that enhance the sense of openness rather than enclosure. At the entrance level, a series of double-height spaces, the atelier, and an exhibition area designate a generous main entrance that also doubles as an open lecture hall.

A deep floor plan creates the opportunity for extensive glass use in the surfaces of the facade. It endows the building with a high degree of generality, offering lavish amounts of light and transparency while maintaining the climate and energy efficiency.

Status
Built

Year
2015

Firm
Tham & Videgård Arkitekter

Firm location
Stockholm, Sweden

Awards Category Typology / Type Institutional: Libraries / Winner Jury

Culture House and Library Allerød, Denmark

The new Culture House and Library in Allerød is an extension and refurbishment of the former Fritz Hansen furniture factory, spanning 23,680 square feet of industrial property.

The Culture House and Library is located in Allerød, north of Copenhagen, and designed by Primus architects in collaboration with Rytter A/S, JPM engineering, and GHB Landscape.

The new library and culture center is an extension and refurbishment of the former Fritz Hansen factory for furniture, and has a total area of 23,680 square feet.

The staggered roof provides ample space and natural light while acknowledging the industrial history of the site. Lighting is integrated into the facade and creates a glowing volume at night.

Status
Built

Year
2015

Firm
Primus Arkitekter

Firm location
Copenhagen, Denmark

Awards Category **Typology** / Type **Institutional: Libraries** / Winner **Popular Choice**

Dokk1 Aarhus, Denmark

Located at the mouth of the Aarhus River, Dokk1 is part of a plan to revitalize the former industrial docks on the harbor by connecting the area to the historic center of the city.

Dokk1 is Scandinavia's largest public library and represents a new generation of modern hybrid libraries. The building is situated at the mouth of the Aarhus River.

Dokk1 is part of an ambitious district plan to revitalize the former industrial cargo docks on the harbor by connecting the area both visually and physically to the historic center of the city.

The principal idea behind the building is a transparent, covered urban space. A large polygonal slice hovers above a glazed prism, which rests on ice-flake-shaped stairs fanning out to the edge of the sea. The ice flakes create wide plateaus and accommodate recreational activities and outdoor events. The building has no clear front or back, as emphasized by the multi-edged top slice that creates the impression of rotation and movement.

The top slice contains media administration and offices for rent. The glass building below allows passersby visual access to the activities in the building while the users have a 360-degree panoramic view from inside. The library contains several divisions in staggered levels that cover literature and media, exhibitions, a children's theater, interactive activities, public events, cafés, and restaurants.

Status
Built

Year
2015

Firm
schmidt hammer lassen architects

Firm location
Copenhagen, Denmark

Awards Category Typology / Type Institutional: Unbuilt Institutional / Winner Jury

Mizengo Pinda Asali & Nyuki Sanctuary — Beekeeping & Education Center
Dodoma, Tanzania

The plans for this sanctuary—dedicated to providing a facility for sustainable honey production and community fostering—include mud-fire brick constructions to be made on-site.

Mizengo Pinda Asali & Nyuki Sanctuary is a honey (asali), beekeeping (nyuki), and education center. The intention of the sanctuary is to provide a centralized facility for honey extraction and processing, a public market, and education and services to local villages in support of beekeeping activities. By teaching sustainable methods, providing resources and a market for harvested products, the government hopes to provide a means of economic support to rural communities. A key goal of the design is to help foster a sense of community, collaboration, and improvement through informal and formal spaces for interaction.

The processing facility will be built to USDA and EU guidelines for global distribution, and profits will return to the Asali and Nyuki Sanctuary to encourage local learning, conservation, and eco-tourism. The sanctuary is organized in a cellular-patterned structure around garden courts providing a framework for future expansion as well as spaces for informal interaction and learning.

The building will use sustainable and locally sourced materials and labor. The structural components include mud-fired bricks that are made on-site. The custom brick bond is dimensional, textural, and interwoven, recalling local weaving traditions.

Status
Concept

Year
2018

Firm
Jaklitsch/Gardner Architects

Firm location
New York, NY, USA

Awards Category Typology / Type **Institutional: Unbuilt Institutional** / Winner **Popular Choice**

The Choice School Thiruvalla, India

The Choice School reimagines school architecture in India and offers a prototype that will help revitalize rural communities and empower future generations.

The new educational community, the Choice School, reimagines school architecture in India, creating a prototype that will help revitalize rural communities and empower future generations. The Choice School takes advantage of defined and focused spaces for learning and development as well as transitional spaces to encourage interaction.

Building on the close-knit society of rural India, the prototype houses grades one through twelve in one building, fostering relationships between students of different ages and allowing for a continuum of learning.

Taking cues from the region's cultural and climatic contexts, the new Choice School mirrors the landscape of Southern India, reinforcing the sense of identity among students, faculty, and the community. Specific influences include the Kerala House Boat; local materials such as stone, clay tiles, and Palmyra Palm; the area's use of vibrant color and texture; and the region's wide range of weather conditions.

Fusing these cultural and geographic elements with modern sustainable technologies and practices situates the Choice School in its contemporary context. The prototype's modularity will allow the Choice School to build additional campuses that adapt to varying sites and local programmatic differences while maintaining its core principles and functions.

Status
Under Construction

Year
2017

Firm
Cetra Ruddy

Firm location
New York, NY, USA

Awards Category Typology / Type **Institutional: Government & Municipal Buildings** / Winner **Popular Choice**

Crematorium in Wo Hop Shek Hong Kong

This design redefines the image of a crematorium by revisiting the needs of grieving families throughout the funeral process and building around this priority to respect the hardships of human life.

A dynamic form with juxtaposed elements merges into the hillside in the rural setting of Wo Hop Shek in Hong Kong. This piece of architecture redefines the image of a crematorium in Hong Kong with reflecting ponds and large tilted lawns.

In the old days, crematoriums were designed based on functional needs. In this project, the genuine need of the grieving families throughout the funeral process was revisited and became the first priority of the design.

By locating the cremation room one floor below the halls, the architects change the backdrop of the alta—it now becomes a natural bamboo yard instead of a curtain. The halls are provided with independent entrances and exits, individual toilets and "joss paper" burners to avoid confrontation with the next grieving family.

After the ceremony, the visitors are directed to a central landscaped garden. A pond there symbolizes the birth of human life. A little waterfall creates the sounds of nature to help calm the mind. An asymmetric approach with vigorous forms symbolizes the variant hardships of human life.

Status
Built

Year
2012

Firm
Architectural Services Department

Firm location
Hong Kong

Awards Category Typology / Type Landscape & Planning: Public Park / Winner Jury

Barangaroo Reserve Sydney, Australia

The Barangaroo Reserve, encompassing twenty-two hectares, undergoes a a redevelopment of its public realm, transforming a huge expanse of empty concrete into humane and usable spaces.

In 2009 PWP Landscape Architecture, in association with Johnson Pilton Walker, developed a public space strategy for the Barangaroo Reserve, a stimulating network of new landmarks on Sydney's waterfront named after a powerful woman of historical importance in Sydney's indigenous culture. Encompassing twenty-two hectares directly west of the Central Business District and the Rocks, Barangaroo has three precincts: Barangaroo South, a mix of office and residential; Barangaroo Central, a mixed-use space with large areas for programmed entertainment; and Barangaroo Reserve, the recreation of a six-hectare "Club Cape" headland that restores the visual geography of Sydney Harbour.

Guided by geomorphologic studies, historical maps, and early paintings, PWP led the design of the headland, including a foreshore constructed from 10,000 large sandstone blocks excavated directly from the site. Pedestrian and bicycle pathways are separated by a low, three-foot-wide sandstone wall.

Barangaroo Reserve transforms a huge expanse of concrete into humane, usable space with ecological goals always in sight. All plantings are native to the Sydney area. Barangaroo has been selected as one of seventeen sites worldwide to participate in the Clinton Climate Initiative Development Program, with the goal of reducing on-site CO_2 emissions to zero.

Status
Built

Year
2015

Firm
PWP Landscape Architecture

Firm location
Berkeley, CA, USA

Awards Category **Typology** / Type **Landscape & Planning: Public Park** / Winner **Popular Choice**

Philadelphia Navy Yards Central Green Philadelphia, PA, USA

A "social ring" sits at the heart of this re-adapted site of wetlands framing a flowering interior park featuring a hammock grove, an outdoor conference room, game courts, and amphitheater.

Once a collection of wetlands and meadows, the 5.5-acre Central Green site at the heart of the Philadelphia Navy Yard is becoming one of the city's most innovative and progressive neighborhoods. The design of Central Green unites the cutting-edge urban potential of the site with its native habitat, resulting in a new type of environment that is sustainable, verdant, social, active, and urban. A twenty-foot-wide "social ring" organizes the site's circulation and frames a unique, immersive interior park featuring specimen trees, flowering meadows, a hammock grove, an outdoor conference room, bocce courts, games tables, fitness stations, and an outdoor amphitheater.

Central Green is the first major public space designed to support the commercial and residential growth at the Navy Yard. It functions as a catalyst for development and an incubator for innovation as it instigates social interaction and exchange. The design re-envisions the office park as a rich mix of active spaces that remain flexible and inviting for a wide spectrum of social uses, activities, and events.

Status
Built

Year
2015

Firm
James Corner Field Operations

Firm location
New York, NY, USA

Awards Category Typology / Type Landscape & Planning: Private Garden / Winner Jury & Popular Choice

Meditation Pavilion & Garden Geneva, Switzerland

A pavilion cantilevers over the lawn and pool of this private garden, while flanking mounds conceal it within the landscape.

The Meditation Pavilion & Garden blends in with the overall conception of the park where its placed, enhancing the composition with its own qualities.

The mounds around the pavilion and the pool create a fluid vegetal belt, changing colors and movements with the seasons, and hiding the pavilion from direct views—allowing only partial or indirect perceptions.

Special attention is given to lighting design, both natural and artificial, in order to preserve the site's intimate character. In both of the pavilion's lateral volumes skylights allow natural light in, while suspended spotlights and indirect lighting enhance the rhythm of the timber cladding and the ceiling's corners.

The pavilion itself is composed of a crossing, central void flanked by those two lateral volumes. The ensemble sits on top of a wooden platform cantilevered over the lawn and pool. The structure is made of V4A stainless steel covered by thermo-coated solid ash wood in walls, floors, and ceilings.

The central void includes two slight reinforcements on the floor in an asymmetric position, and can be closed by sliding elements from inside the walls.

Status
Built

Year
2012

Firm
GM Architectes Associés

Firm location
Geneva, Switzerland

Awards Category Typology / Type Landscape & Planning: Unbuilt Masterplan / Winner Jury

Rethinking Refugee Communities

A new toolkit for UNHCR to plan and design refugee settlements and improve communities' health, safety, nutrition, and access to education.

More than 19.5 million refugees are dispersed across the globe, many living in camps averaging a stay of seventeen years. Ennead Architects partnered with Stanford University and the United Nations High Commissioner for Refugees (UNHCR) to help UNHCR meet its commitment to "enable refugees to access and live in dignity in secure settlements that improve their social, economic, and environmental quality of life as a community."

The toolkit is a systematic framework for integrating information, design, technical tools, and expertise of multiple disciplines and stakeholders to better plan settlements. This framework operates in three physical scales: macro, meso, and micro, and in five stages of camp evolution: contingency, emergency, transition, durable, and exit phases.

The toolkit will enable UNHCR to plan and design refugee settlements in a more holistic manner by improving the selection process for potential camp sites and by defining the means to link refugee and host communities for their mutual benefit.

The toolkit will benefit refugees by improving their health, safety, nutrition, and access to education and economic opportunity. It will benefit host communities by leveraging the economy and aid that camps can offer.

Status
Concept

Firm
Ennead Architects

Firm location
New York, NY, USA

Awards Category **Typology** / Type **Landscape & Planning: Unbuilt Masterplan** / Winner **Popular Choice**
Yenikapi Transfer Point and Archaeo-Park Area Istanbul, Turkey

For a better articulation of urban space, Tabanlioglu Architects imagines a network of sunken plazas and underground connections to relate elements of the city surface.

In Yenikapi, infrastructure is ideal in terms of function, yet what is missing is the articulation of urban space as a method of styling the joints in between formal elements. Avoiding imposing an icon, the structure is not dominant but considered one of the many elements in building the space. The objects of urban living integrate seamlessly with sunken public piazzas.

Yenikapi becomes the nexus of all underground connections related to the city surface with this plan for lower piazzas created under a semi-permeable roof system. That protective shield designates the space and the permeable elements filter the daylight into the sunken piazzas, creating a feeling of spaciousness, exploring new possibilities of contemporary temples where people meet.

A stroller's curiosity is first piqued by the display units of the City Archive, located in the piazza. The main expedition area is designed as the site museum with the units of exhibition stretched towards the Archeo-Park area. The museum is designed in related units that may be visited separately or in a cohesive order.

Status
Concept

Firm
Tabanlioglu Architects

Firm location
Istanbul, Turkey

Awards Category Typology / Type Transportation: Bus & Train Stations / Winner Jury

Arnhem Central Master Plan Arnhem, The Netherlands

The master plan for Arnhem's transport hub focuses on optimizing pedestrian accessibility and integrating sustainable features such as heat and cold storage and an underground waste management system.

Arnhem Central Master Plan is a large urban plan development composed of diverse elements which constitute a vibrant transport hub. The architecture responds to the natural sloping landscape of Arnhem, while adding to the iconography of the city.

More than 65,000 people pass through the station area every day. This expansion generates 861,110 square feet of office space, 118,400 square feet of shops, 150 housing units, a cinema complex, a bus terminal, a new station hall, a fourth railway platform, a railway underpass, a car tunnel, storage for 4,500 bicycles, and a 1,000-car garage. The terminal building serves as a linking node between these facilities and the city center.

With a focus on finding overlapping areas of shared parameters and common values, movement studies formed the cornerstone of the proposal. These studies resulted in the intersection of different traffic systems being reduced to a minimum in order to optimize pedestrian accessibility to all facilities.

The complete plan is designed with sustainable features in mind, with heat and cold storage, multiple ground use, an underground waste transportation system, and a unified utility tunnel incorporated into the design.

Status
Built

Year
2015

Firm
UNStudio

Firm location
Amsterdam, The Netherlands

Awards Category Typology / Type Transportation: Airports / Winner Jury
Heydar Aliyev International Airport Baku, Azerbaijan

Istanbul-based Autoban reinvents the interior architecture and experiential design of a terminal in Azerbaijan's international airport.

The new landmark terminal at Azerbaijan's Heydar Aliyev International Airport features interior architecture and experiential design by Istanbul-based Autoban. Bearing all the hallmarks of the multidisciplinary studio's experimental, genre-defying approach, the contemporary interiors overturn airport conventions of cavernous space and impersonal experience.

Taking inspiration from Azerbaijani hospitality, Autoban's Red Dot award-winning design spans the entirety of the terminal's passenger spaces, and includes striking custom-made wooden "cocoons" that create a sense of welcome and discovery, and opportunities to either meet or retreat.

This use of narrative and unconventional use of forms is typical of Autoban's idiosyncratic approach. For more than a decade, the studio has developed a reputation for its imaginative, human approach to design, creating spaces that are firmly rooted in cultural, social, and geographic narratives. At Heydar Aliyev, the bespoke furnishings and lighting schemes defy airport typologies with tactile natural materials such as wood, stone, and textiles. The cocoons, which vary in size and house an array of cafés, kiosks, and other amenities, exist at the convergence of architecture and art, creating an intriguing landscape within the huge transportation hub, and challenging expectations of the airport environment.

Status
Built

Year
2014

Firm
Autoban

Firm location
Istanbul, Turkey

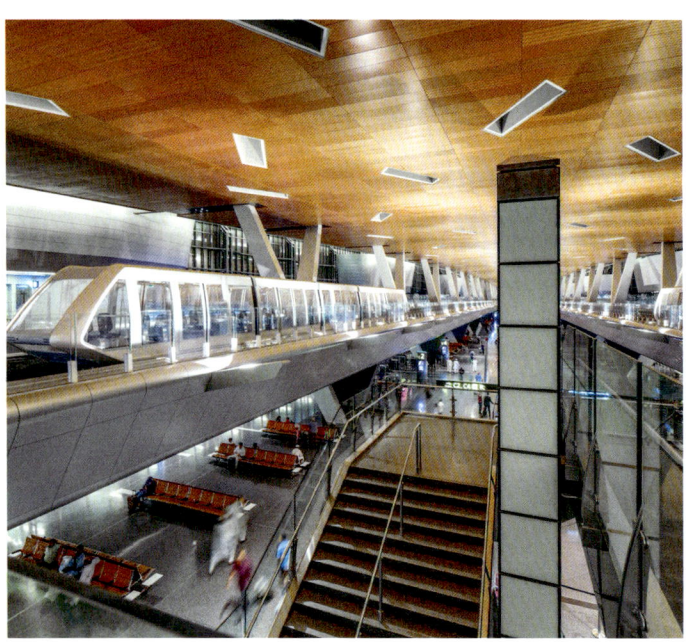

Awards Category **Typology** / Type **Transportation: Airports** / Winner **Popular Choice**
Hamad International Airport Doha, Qatar

In the design of the Hamad International Airport, materials were selected for longevity, sustainability, and local significance.

The design of the passenger terminal complex at Qatar's new airport celebrates form, surface, and light while providing an efficient yet inspirational experience for travelers. As the landmark home for Qatar Airways, the country's national airline, the terminal can accommodate thirty million passengers annually and has forty-one unrestricted contact gates.

Departing passengers experience an undulating roof in the light-filled departure hall. The steel-framed glass wall provides unobstructed views from the curbside arrival area through the ticketing hall, enabling passengers to easily find their destinations. The longer east and west facades have similar high-performance glass that controls solar heat gain and glare.

A vast wood ceiling in the longest concourse provides visual warmth that contrasts with the sleek metal and glass surfaces. In other concourses, vaulted metal ceilings mimic the undulating roofline. Glass envelops the spacious hold rooms, quiet rooms, passenger activity nodes, and seventeen airline lounges. Skylights and interconnecting glass ceiling "zippers" provide daylighting and dramatic evening desert views.

Status
Built

Year
2014

Firm
HOK

Firm location
San Francisco, CA, USA

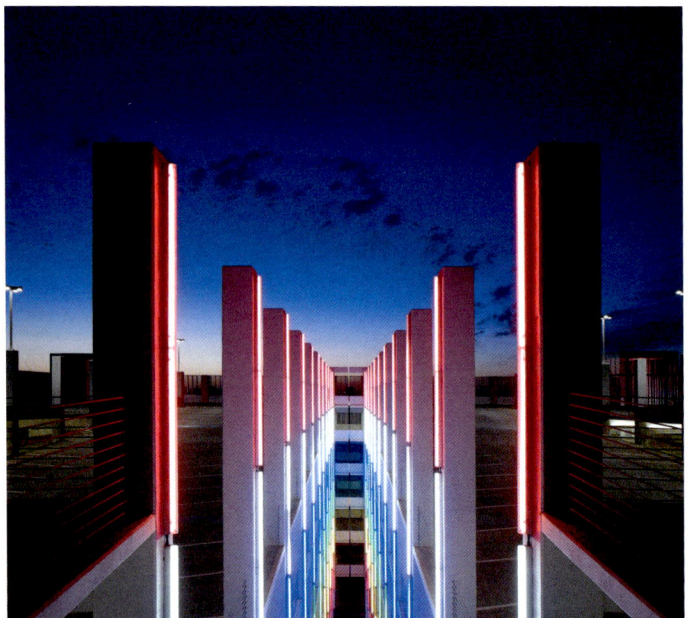

Awards Category Typology / Type Transportation: Parking Structures / Winner Jury

Chesapeake Car Park 4 Oklahoma City, OK, USA

A graceful and textured profile, compatible with existing campus architecture, led to the design of Chesapeake Car Park 4.

The project goals of Chesapeake Car Park 4 include function, safety, a fun experience, and compatibility with existing campus architecture.

Building 15 and Car Park 4 are envisioned as paired structures. The vertical white aluminum fins provide a graceful, textured profile and allow the structure to change from a transparent frontal view to an opaque angular view.

Safety features include key card access to the garage at both the automobile entry and the pedestrian entry. Additionally, there is plenty of light to navigate the space, and there are security stations with panic buttons, security cameras, elevator phones, ample exterior lighting, and a glass wall in the elevator facing campus.

Status
Built

Year
2015

Firm
Elliott + Associates

Firm location
Oklahoma City, OK, USA

Awards Category Typology / Type Transportation: Parking Structures / Winner Popular Choice

May–September Indianapolis, IN, USA

Rob Ley Studio challenges the notion of the parking structure as an unappreciated piece of infrastructure and transforms the Eskenazi Hospital parking structure with an articulated and dynamic facade.

This project began with an interest in challenging the typical notion of the parking structure as an unappreciated infrastructural typology by transforming the new Eskenazi Hospital parking structure into an interactive, synthetic terrain.

A field of 7,000 angled-metal panels in conjunction with an articulated east-west color strategy creates a dynamic facade system that offers observers a unique visual experience depending on their vantage point and the pace at which they are moving through the site. In this way, pedestrians and slow-moving vehicles within close proximity to the hospital will experience a noticeable, dappled shift in color and transparency as they move across the hospital grounds, while motorists driving along West Michigan Street will experience a faster color shift which changes depending on their direction of travel.

Status
Built

Year
2014

Firm
Rob Ley Studio

Firm location
Los Angeles, CA, USA

Awards Category **Typology** / Type **Transportation: Marinas & Ports** / Winner **Jury**

Beale Street Landing Memphis, TN, USA

The project for Beale Street Landing proposes a five-acre qualified public space in order to bring the community to the riverside.

Beale Street Landing's intent was to create a landmark capable of reconnecting Tom Lee Park, the historic cobblestones, the Blues coming down Beale Street, and the Mississippi River. The project proposes a five-acre qualified public space in order to bring the community back to the riverside.

The project tries to be gentle with the riverfront by designing a topographic landscape with smooth and curved geometries, while extending Tom Lee Park over the terminal building to minimize its impact.

RTN's goal was to celebrate the river, therefore most of their design solutions reflect this concept. Visitors are able to see the river from everywhere with no interference. As such, the architects minimized all vertical and obstructing elements, and the terminal building is surrounded entirely with a clear storefront to allow river views. As another way to celebrate the river, the terminal building service core, which penetrates the roof, was wrapped with a photo of the river during sunset. The image is pixelated in twenty colors and built with aluminum-colored panels.

The docking facility area is formed by a bridge, a helical ramp—resembling the nineteenth-century paddle wheelers—and a floating pontoon.

Status
Built

Year
2014

Firm
RTN

Firm location
Caba, Argentina

Awards Category Typology / Type **Transportation: Marinas & Ports** / Winner **Popular Choice**

OneOcean Marina Port Vell Barcelona, Spain

Aiming to connect the industrial port and the old town of Barcelona, this project involves the landscape management of 170,000 square feet of quayside to improve service to an increasing number of cruising yachts.

OneOcean Port Vell Marina in Barcelona extends and improves facilities in order to provide service to an increasing number of cruising yachts. The project involves the construction of two buildings on the water and the landscape management of 170,000 square feet of quayside.

The general strategy of the project aims to achieve the integration of the new buildings and the public space within their singular environment—halfway between the industrial port and the old town of Barcelona.

A single unifying approach achieves an image of order and continuity. The large area occupied by the docks and floating quays must remain free for use and space reasons; the new lightning, signposting, and vegetation are designed with this in mind.

The buildings are covered by a lattice that has been specially designed for this project. The OneOcean Club is comprised of a restaurant and a cocktail bar, which are organized into two structures joined together under a large lattice. The Gallery building accommodates offices for the management companies that operate in the marinas. This structure is a two-floor building located on a platform over water.

Status
Built

Year
2014

Firm
SCOB Architecture & Landscape

Firm location
Barcelona, Spain

Awards Category **Typology** / Type **Transportation: Highways & Bridges** / Winner **Jury**

The Bicycle Bridge Across the Sava River Bohinjska Bistrica, Slovenia

Part of a bicycle path that connects the Bohinjska Bistrica village with a nearby lake, this bridge uses traditional architecture and materials as a basis for quality infrastructure.

The Bicycle Bridge Across the Sava River is part of the bicycle path that connects Bohinjska Bistrica village with the Bohinj Lake. The bridge is attractive and functional while complementing the sensitive environment of the Bohinj area. The choice of materials, inventive structure, and architectural design itself contribute to the feeling that the bridge belongs there.

It spans the river in a long, elegant curve. The Sava is a river with a fluctuating rate of water flow, so the span and geometry of the bridge have to accommodate accordingly. The width and the slope of the bridge reflect its use as a bike path. Spanning 180 feet, it sits on both banks, supported by two V-shaped concrete piers, permitting the slim and rational design. The bridge is constructed out of two laminated timber girders, which serve also as railings. The timber girders are made of laminated spruce and protected by a coating of larch boards and shingles. Timber is a logical choice of building material in the region, while the method of stacking wood siding and use of shingles are a contemporary interpretation of traditional regional architectural ideas.

Status
Built

Year
2013

Firm
dans arhitekti

Firm location
Ljubljana, Slovenia

Awards Category **Typology** / Type **Transportation: Highways & Bridges** / Winner **Popular Choice**

SFC Bridge Toronto, ON, Canada

The SFC bridge, part of Toronto's underground PATH network, demonstrates how creative collaborations between artists, architects, and private developers can bring unprecedented experiences to urban infrastructure.

The SFC Bridge, designed by artists Jennifer Marman and Daniel Borins in collaboration with architect James Khamsi, demonstrates how creative collaborations can bring unprecedented experiences to urban infrastructure. As cities collaborate with private developments to bring pedestrian access to areas dominated by industrial and transportation infrastructure, making sustainable and vibrant access is a typical challenge. Completed in February, 2015, the project combines public art and architecture to transform a pedestrian access point into a striking landmark.

The SFC bridge is part of Toronto's underground PATH network, which recently expanded aboveground to create year-round elevated walkways over rail lines and under expressways in the area south of Union Station. Sloping upwards from the Delta Hotel, the bridge takes a 120-degree turn to connect with the existing Convention Centre SkyWalk (built in 1989).

Dark aluminum panels wrap the bridge's exterior, following its structural trusses, to bind its integral slopes and bends. Between the bands, triangular windows cast shapes of light on the bridge's interior. Stimulating the curiosity of passersby, they frame views of the urban backdrop, visually connecting pedestrians to the city.

Status
Built

Year
2015

Firm
Marman-Borins-Khamsi

Firm location
New York, NY, USA

Awards Category **Typology** / Type **Transportation: Unbuilt Transportation** / Winner **Jury**

Stockholm Airport City Stockholm, Sweden

Anticipating a rise in travel demand, this imagined master plan for the Stockholm Airport City fully integrates the infrastructure of the airport with the city in which it is based.

This project imagines a time when aviation technology might be advanced enough that aircraft, airports, and cities could coexist. Airport systems join city systems as part of the city's infrastructure, including micro-termini, citywide baggage systems, and shorter runways that slot into the urban context. The project is based in Stockholm, one of the fastest growing cities in Europe, where a testing ground is established to create a fully integrated urban airport.

Travel demand in the aviation industry is set to double by 2030, and in order to satisfy that demand and address the increasing importance of the airport in local economies, capacity in the industry needs to increase. Airports have suffered under the strain of this increasing demand and have become isolated processing stations. The negative effects of aviation on the environment, and necessary security measures and maintenance have caused this isolation.

Airports need to adapt themselves to become more attractive gateways and capture as much of the growing air traffic demand as possible to in turn drive their local economies

Status
Concept

Firm
Alex Sutton

Firm location
London, UK

Awards Category **Typology** / Type **Transportation: Unbuilt Transportation** / Winner **Popular Choice**

LaGuardia Airport Master Plan New York, NY, USA

SHoP imagines a master plan for New York's LaGuardia Airport that would eliminate truck traffic on local streets, embedding environmental responsibility and efficiency into the design of this transportation hub.

In 2015, SHoP was selected as a finalist in the Master Plan Design Competition for New York's LaGuardia Airport (LGA). The goal was to reimagine the entirety of LGA as a world-class facility, offering a unified terminal environment, improved airside and landside operations, and an appropriate gateway to New York City.

The approaches to LGA were entirely reconceived to eliminate truck traffic on local streets, resulting in improved clarity and convenience for drivers entering from the adjacent highway. Two shoreside parks with soft tidal edges were proposed as part of a comprehensive approach to environmental responsibility that also included installations of facade-integrated solar technology and an on-site power plant designed to back up the community grid in case of emergency.

Responding to LaGuardia's history of delays due to tarmac crowding, SHoP also proposed the gates be arranged around two island concourses. In order to encourage pedestrian line-of-sight way-finding clarity between all parts of the complex—and to achieve related improvements in passenger flow—the plan uses bridges rather than tunnels to cross the proposed taxiways.

Status
Concept

Firm
SHoP Architects

Firm location
New York, NY, USA

Awards Category **Plus** / Type **Architecture + Art** / Winner **Jury**
Fogo Island Artist Studios Fogo Island, NL, Canada

Six sustainable, off-the-grid artist studios are built at various locations on scenic Fogo Island in Canada.

The Shorefast Foundation and the Fogo Island Arts Corporation commissioned Todd Saunders to design a series of six artist studios on various Fogo Island locations. These organizations are committed to preserving the islanders' traditions and aim to rejuvenate the island through arts and culture.

The Bridge Studio is dramatically located on a steep hillside overlooking the calm waters of an inland pond. The Tower Studio is situated on a stretch of rocky coastline in Shoal Bay. The Fogo Island Squish Studio is located just outside the small town of Tilting on the eastern end of Fogo Island.

All six studios are 100 percent off the grid with no connection to public services. In the Long Studio, all heat is produced from solar panels on the roof and a small wood stove. Rainwater is collected from the roof and stored in tanks in concealed storage rooms to provide water for the shower and small kitchen. In addition, a composting toilet is installed and all excess gray water is treated inside the building.

Status
Built

Year
2012

Firm
Saunders Architecture

Firm location
Bergen, Norway

Awards Category **Plus** / Type **Architecture + Collaboration** / Winner **Jury & Popular Choice**

Alpine Shelter — A Room With a View Mountain Skuta, Slovenia

A student-designed alpine shelter in Slovenia is built to withstand harsh climate conditions with minimal maintenance.

This project was developed by an architectural design studio at the Harvard Graduate School of Design, AKT II, and OFIS. Thirteen students faced the challenge of designing an innovative yet practical shelter that meets the needs of the extreme alpine climate. Inspired by the vernacular architecture of Slovenia, with its rich and diverse architectural heritage, the selected bivouac is a response to the harsh conditions of wind, snow, landslides, and terrain.

The outer shell is realized with öko skin, as the concrete slats withstand extreme mountain conditions and offer long-term resistance. Concrete is made from natural materials and its authentic appearance blends in with the surrounding landscape and mountains. The alpine shelter is located on Mountain Skuta in Slovenia. Its position within the wilderness respects natural resources and has minimal impact on the ground.

One of the challenges the architects faced was to build a bivouac capable of withstanding harsh weather conditions. As the site is extremely hard to access, another important aspect was to keep maintenance to a minimum, especially for the facade.

Status
Built

Year
2015

Firm
Rieder Smart Elements

Firm location
Maishofen, Austria

Awards Category **Plus** / Type **Architecture + Branding** / Winner **Jury**

The Strand — Environmental Graphics San Francisco, CA, USA

A derelict movie house in San Francisco is transformed into a theater, rehearsal space, and headquarters for a nonprofit theater company.

The Strand, a once derelict movie house in San Francisco, has been transformed into a second home for the city's preeminent nonprofit theater company, American Conservatory Theater.

The redefined space houses an intimate proscenium theater, educational facilities, a public lobby and café, and a black-box theater and rehearsal space. The program is inserted within the shell of the former 725-seat cinema, overlaying essential modern theater elements on top of the raw backdrop of the original building.

As part of the renovation, a graphic identity was developed for the Strand, a fifty-year-old institution, tailored to reflect the new space and its mission. Focused on new work, emerging artists, arts education, and community outreach, the Strand's visual identity had to convey the unadorned immediacy of experimental theater and reflect the gritty, transitional aspects of the surrounding neighborhood.

The stencil, a staple of backstage labeling, was used to express the direct, stripped-down simplicity of the Strand's space and program. This theme was carried throughout the building's environmental graphics and signage, including the exterior blade and canopy, interior way-finding, and donor wall. Lettering and pictograms were painted directly on the walls or cut into metal sheets to resemble industrial stencil sets.

Status
Built

Year
2015

Firm
Skidmore, Owings & Merrill

Firm location
San Francisco, CA, USA

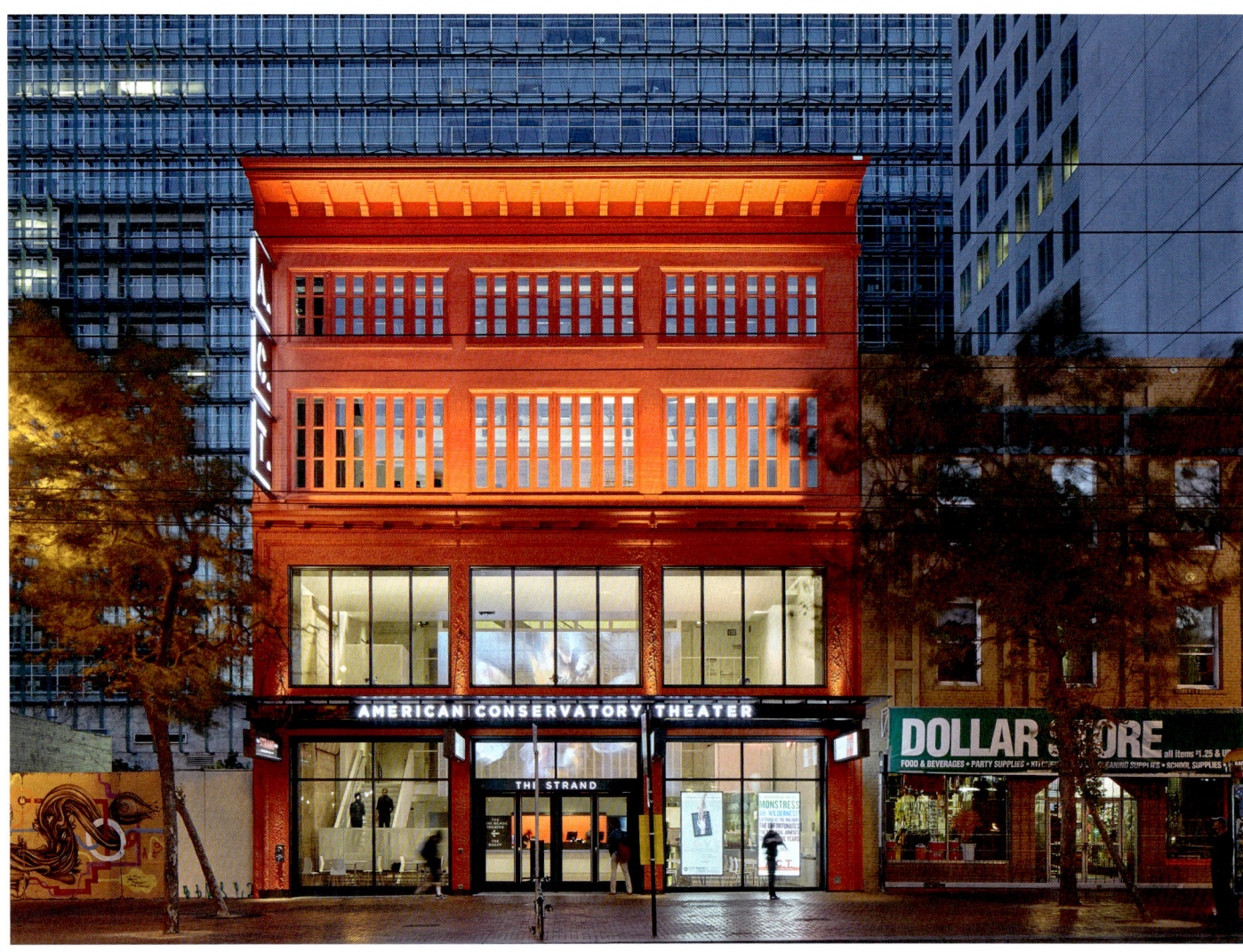

Awards Category **Plus** / Type **Architecture + Branding** / Winner **Popular Choice**
Adidas Boston Marathon Runbase Boston, MA, USA

Located near the finish line of the iconic race, the Adidas Boston Marathon Runbase marks a new center for Boston's urban running scene.

Part locker room, part Adidas store, and part museum, the Adidas Boston Marathon Runbase is a prototype retail experience located a few feet from the finish line of the iconic race. The experience is a collaborative effort between Adidas, one of the marathon's major sponsors, the Boston Athletic Association, the race's organizer, and Marathon Sports, the local running store.

    The store design takes advantage of the joint venture, becoming a new center for Boston's urban running scene. A new merchandise display system places state-of-the-art running gear in a historical context, alongside vitrines containing artifacts from the race's storied history. An interactive database and leaderboard turn Boston's runners into a community, making the base a natural place to start club runs, extending the store experience into the city. The store also features lockers, showers, and a recovery area for runners and finishers.

Status
Built

Year
2015

Firm
Parc Office

Firm location
New York, NY, USA

Awards Category **Plus** / Type **Architecture + Communication** / Winner **Jury**

TalkBox Staten Island, Newark, and Other U.S. Cities

TalkBox is a community outreach platform housed in an aluminum payphone structure, designed to give voice to underrepresented audiences in partnership with news organizations.

In close collaboration with the flagship public radio station WNYC, SHoP Architects developed, designed, and fabricated a prototype for a nontraditional community outreach platform. The goal, supported by a grant from the Knight Foundation, was to create an easily reproducible system that could become a model for other news organizations nationwide, a means to involve underrepresented audiences in their programming.

Housed within a standard aluminum payphone enclosure, TalkBox can be installed directly on city streets. WNYC and SHoP worked to give TalkBox a form that would be visually striking, perform robustly on city streets, and invite users to tell their most intimate stories. The design is meant to evoke recording studio soundproofing, to suggest the importance of each individual's voice. By lifting the handset, locals who might not usually listen to the news—much less record it—can be drawn into and empowered to participate in important civic conversations that otherwise take place only on air.

TalkBox was deployed for the first time in July of 2015 at the St. George terminal of the Staten Island Ferry, where it was used to solicit community reactions on the first anniversary of Eric Garner's death. The device brought out powerful commentary.

Status
Built

Year
2015

Firm
SHoP Architects

Firm location
New York, NY, USA

Awards Category **Plus** / Type **Architecture + Communication** / Winner **Popular Choice**

Tubular Baitasi Beijing, China

People's Architecture Office designs an interactive facade of periscopes for the public to peer both into the building and beyond the building towards other Beijing monuments.

Tubular Baitasi is a visitor center and event and exhibition space showcasing regeneration strategies for the Baitasi historic district during Beijing Design Week. The center is housed in a multi-story building that uses ubiquitous HVAC metal ducts as a type of architectural vernacular.

The design of the facade aims to engage the public in various ways. The facade features a sign that spells out the Chinese word for "White Pagoda Temple," ensuring the main entrance to the neighborhood is visible from a distance. Integrated into the sign are periscopes that link the street front to other locations. Passersby can look into the ducts and find views of the 700 year-old White Pagoda Temple and the People's Commune Building, a 1950s experimental housing complex. The ducts also extend out from the building onto the sidewalk to form public seating.

The facade also connects the public with the interior through one periscope that peers into the second floor of the building to show the teaching space of the Architecture Association and a 3D print shop. The interior includes exhibition spaces and an auditorium furnished with ducts made into donut-shaped seating, stools, adjustable tables, and panel displays.

Status
Built

Year
2015

Firm
People's Architecture Office

Firm location
Beijing, China

Awards Category **Plus** / Type **Architecture + Community, + Humanitarianism** / Winner **Jury**

Thread: Artists' Residency and Cultural Center Sinthian, Senegal

This design—a collaborative cultural facility that provides communal gathering spaces and housing for artist residencies in a remote Senegalese community—uses local materials and construction methods.

Situated in the community of Sinthian, Senegal, this project offers programs for the community, including a waiting space for a medical clinic, gathering space, and residency for visiting artists. A collaboration with privately funded medical NGOs that have operated in the area for more than twenty years, the cultural facility is intended to complement the existing clinics. The facility provides a common ground within a community consisting of twelve tribes.

A parametric transformation of the traditional pitched roof is achieved through a process of inversion, inscribing a series of courtyards within the plan of the building and simultaneously creating shaded studio areas around the perimeter of the courtyard. The inverted roof provides an optimum solution for collection and storage of rainwater. With a total footprint of 11,285 square feet, the project is capable of supplementing substantial domestic and agricultural water for the community.

Relying exclusively on local materials and construction techniques, the building's traditional structure is formed primarily of large bamboo members and compressed earth blocks. Climatic considerations figure prominently into the building's form and specify the orientation of the studios. The building offers ample shading of outdoor areas and considers wind orientation for optimum ventilation.

Status
Built

Year
2015

Firm
Toshiko Mori Architect

Firm location
New York, NY, USA

Awards Category Plus / Type Architecture + Low Cost Housing / Winner Jury & Popular Choice

Doctors' Housing for Partners in Health Rwinkwavu, Rwanda

This sustainable housing project in Rwanda responds to climate conditions, local needs, and traditional building methods.

Working in partnership with Rwandan Village Enterprises (RVE) for Partners In Health and the Rwandan Ministry of Health, the architects created the first comprehensive urban planning document for rural Rwinkwavu.

The first built phase of this project is the "Share Houses," offering 6,900 square feet of housing for hospital staff. The design responds to its site on a hot, dry hillside, to tight budget requirements, and to a desire to enhance connections between staff and community by creating "a village within a village."

Each bedroom has its own private exterior space facing the views of the valley with a large overhang for rain and heat protection. The bedrooms are connected to the shared bathrooms and common spaces with a covered screened exterior walkway, which provides a sense of enclosure and privacy for residents and also a connection to more traditional ways of building.

All construction materials were sourced from within Rwanda, with most coming from the neighboring areas. Local stone was quarried for all foundations and walkways. A neighborhood women's cooperative was employed to make all the handmade bricks for wall construction. A ventilated roof cavity is clad with clay tiles for thermal and acoustic performance.

Status
Built

Year
2015

Firm
Sharon Davis Design

Firm location
New York, NY, USA

Awards Category Plus / Type Architecture + Community, + Living Small / Winner Jury & Popular Choice

Humble Hostel Beijing, China

A design solution providing a 130-square-foot adjustable room that aims to retain communal space in Beijing's "hutong" neighborhoods.

Nowadays in Beijing most of the courtyard properties are divided up into mixed occupants. Everyone is trying to occupy more space, thus the shared communal space in the middle has shrunk.

The purpose of this design is to give back space to the communal courtyard and provide space for its neighbors. The solution was to install a sliding wall made up of windows, doors, and storage cupboards on the front of the hostel. The wall can slide back and forth so that the proportion of indoor and outdoor space can be adjusted based on need.

This adaptable design creates breathing space within a chaotic Beijing courtyard life. The area can be used for public leisure, a tearoom, a chess room, a bar, or bicycle storage.

The hostel is located in Beijing's historic Dashilar neighborhood—one of the few remaining areas of those ancient alleyways and courtyards known as "hutongs." This 130-square-foot room integrates three beds, a workspace, and a small bathroom.

With more rooms being built up, more space will be given back to the courtyard. As the living environment improves, the aging community can also be infused with a vibrant neighborhood atmosphere.

Status
Built

Year
2015

Firm
CaoPu studio

Firm location
Beijing, China

Awards Category **Plus** / Type **Architecture + Living Small** / Winner **Popular Choice**

ATLAS Tiny House Longmont, CO, USA

ATLAS is a mobile habitat system that utilizes natural resources and minimizes dependence on the grid by collecting rain water, using solar power, and implementing passive cooling and heating.

ATLAS was invented in order to answer one critical question: how can a mobile structure create a habitat that blends the experience of the environment with the power of the environment.

This crossover RV/Tiny House utilizes natural resources and minimizes dependence on the grid by collecting rain water, using solar power, and implementing passive cooling and heating.

The living space is expanded outdoors with a fold-down deck and a fold-up shade awning that fits sleekly in the frame. The wall revealed behind the transformational deck/awning is entirely glass. The windows in this wall open up to the kitchen and create a bar for serving food and drinks in the interior and exterior.

The angle of the deck creates the largest footprint near the entrance, utilizing the largest hinge space. The awning shape angles inversely to the slope of the roof, providing shade over the bar and the highest section of glass.

In the interior a full set of stairs is used instead of a ship ladder traditionally seen in small spaces. Under the stairs storage space glides out, keeping in line with the transformer idea of the whole project.

Status
Built

Year
2015

Firm
F9 Productions Inc

Firm location
Longmont, CO, USA

Awards Category **Plus** / Type **Architecture + Engineering** / Winner **Jury**

Grace Farms New Canaan, CT, USA

This unobtrusive, 83,000-square-foot building in a farmland setting is a complex of glass-walled spaces.

The recently completed River Building for Grace Community Church blends into its natural surroundings, minimally impacting views across what was formerly gently sloping farmland. The 83,000-square-foot building is a complex of glass-walled spaces that includes a sanctuary, a library, a dining hall, a pavilion, and a gymnasium, connected by a sloping, winding roof.

Robert Silman worked closely with the highly regarded structural engineer Mutsuro Sasaki, a frequent collaborator and close colleague of Sejima and Nishizawa of SANAA, during the earliest concept stages of the design. With Silman leading the effort, the two firms created a close and effective relationship that led to a structural approach celebrating SANAA's understated approach while meeting the unique challenges of the project.

Hundreds of "flag pole" steel pipe columns, each individually fixed at their base, provide an overall lateral system that does not require crossing beams to achieve stability. A single glulam type and size was modified throughout to address the specific challenges of the site. This included adding steel to create trusses over long spans and additional outrigger framing at the longer overhangs. Local carpenters were able to build much of the roof structure.

Status
Built

Year
2015

Firm
Robert Silman Associates

Firm location
New York, NY, USA

166

Awards Category **Plus** / Type **Architecture + Engineering, + Wood** / Winner **Jury & Popular Choice**

ZCB Bamboo Pavilion Kowloon Bay, Hong Kong

This 3,765-square-foot public pavilion in Hong Kong has tailor-made white fabric stretched over a bamboo grid-shell constructed with traditional techniques.

The ZCB Bamboo Pavilion is an innovative public event space built in Kowloon Bay, Hong Kong. It is a long-span, bending bamboo grid-shell structure with a footprint of approximately 3,765 square feet and a seating capacity of 200 people. It is used to host exhibitions, performances, and events that promote low-carbon living, construction, and development.

Bamboo is an environmentally friendly, renewable natural resource that is regionally widely available. The project is built from 475 large bamboo poles, bent on-site to shape the structure. The poles are hand-tied together with metal wire using techniques based on the century-old, traditional Cantonese bamboo scaffolding craft. The pavilion is a large diagrid shell structure that is folded down into three hollow columns. These columns rest on three circular concrete footings. A tailor-made white tensile fabric is stretched over the structure and is brightly lit from inside the three legs.

Building the project challenged the boundaries of the architect's design control. Bamboo has widely varying geometric, dimensional, and functional properties, and the scaffolding industry does not use conventional architectural drawings for its intuitive constructions. To deal with these parameters, new methods were developed that merged precise digital design and simulation systems with inconsistent natural resources.

Status
Built

Year
2015

Firm
Chinese University of Hong Kong, School of Architecture

Firm location
Shatin, Hong Kong

Awards Category **Plus** / Type **Architecture + Art** / Winner **Popular Choice**
Petite Vie Québec City, QC, Canada

Built as part of a public art circuit curated by EXMURO arts publics, the design for Petite Vie intends to create a strong form that fits in a passage without directly taking over the surrounding elements.

The Petite Vie was built as part of "Les Passages Insolites," a public art circuit curated by EXMURO arts publics. Without any imposed theme, Fontaine/Fortin/Labelle were asked to invest in a place in the Quartier Création and create an unusual situation.

The design intent was to create a strong form that fit in a passage. Without directly taking over the surrounding elements, formal gestures are intended as a reinterpretation of some typical forms of Old Québec with a postmodern detachment. The facade invites passersby to question their role in the city's architectural landscape.

Francis Fontaine, Luca Fortin, and Pascal Labelle are a creative group of individuals from distinct universes who have worked together since their first encounter at the École d'Architecture de l'Université Laval. Combining their backgrounds in art, engineering, and architecture results in a singular approach towards architecture and design.

Status
Built

Year
2015

Firm
Fontaine/Fortin/Labelle

Firm location
Québec City, QC, Canada

Awards Category **Plus** / Type **Architecture + Learning** / Winner **Jury**

Arckit Dublin, Ireland

Arckit is a new architectural model system that allows users to physically design, build, and modify working models using reusable, modular components.

Arckit is a groundbreaking new architectural model system that allows users to physically design, build, and modify working models radically faster than ever before. Architects can now bring their ideas to life with speed and precision, inspiring spontaneous creativity and a practical approach to designing multiple structures.

Arckit is based on contemporary building techniques, and every component is made to a standard four-foot grid so it can be envisaged at a scale relative to its surroundings. The reusable interconnecting components use no glue and are completely modular, making it possible to create a diverse range of scaled structures that can be used as physical working models to communicate architectural ideas and include clients in the design process.

Arckit components are available digitally within SketchUp and Autodesk Revit for concept builds. Arckit's online Arckitexture image library of finishes supplied by real building companies enables users to dress their completed models. Arckit will be encouraging everyone to participate in the realization of new components.

From renowned architecture practices to university courses, Arckit is fast building a strong reputation as a flexible and creative design tool.

Status
Built

Year
2014

Firm
Arckit

Firm location
Dublin, Ireland

Awards Category **Plus** / Type **Architecture + Learning** / Winner **Popular Choice**

Woodleigh School — Homestead Project Langwarrin South, Australia

The new building for this progressive school, founded in the 1970s on a twenty-hectare bush property, is comprised of spaces that perform in many guises, challenging old and new teaching and learning approaches.

The process of reimagining the Woodleigh School learning environment required a deep understanding of the values and philosophy of the school's origins. Opened in the 1970s on a twenty-hectare bush property, this progressive school emphasizes independent thought.

Homesteads form the core of student life and underpin a unique model of teaching and learning. The time for new homesteads had arrived. A lengthy process of stakeholder engagement and brief analysis was undertaken to ensure the spaces would embody and foster Woodleigh values in their built form.

The homestead spaces are required to perform in many guises, challenging old and new teaching and learning approaches while simultaneously instilling a collegial sense of belonging and ownership. The internal planning, combined with sliding walls and partitioning curtains, generates a variety of contemporary learning settings. These settings facilitate and further the educational demands of the school's curriculum: connected, collaborative, varied, personalized, and environmentally focused learning.

The tactile nature of the materials, including rammed earth, spotted gum timber, exposed concrete floors, and rock, allows the bold gestures of the soaring truss roof, solid mass walls, and folded iron spouts to sit harmoniously within the landscape.

Status
Built

Year
2015

Firm
Law Architects

Firm location
Fitzroy North, Australia

Awards Category **Plus** / Type **Architecture + Light** / Winner **Jury**
Quonochontaug Residence Charlestown, RI, USA

A holiday retreat for a New York family featuring an open-plan ground floor punctuated by double-height, skylit volumes that progress from the entrance to bay views.

The Quonochontaug House in coastal Rhode Island is located three hours from New York and is built as a retreat for a family from Brooklyn. The design is organized around an open-plan ground floor punctuated by a series of double-height skylit spaces that progress from entry to bay view. The light volumes alternate around an east-west axis defined by a pool terrace (to the east) and the ocean bay (to the west). They taper at their apex for precise views of the sky above, and provide shifting and ephemeral natural light patterns throughout the day.

As those who dwell in New York typically experience light, shade, and color as exterior elements, this house harnesses an opportunity to allow sunlight (and moonlight) into the deep interior of the house as something unfamiliar. The house embraces the experience of the sky, one that the owners do not get from their interior experiences of the big city. The light is subtle and constant in terms of colorization and luminosity.

The interior space is delineated by a cluster of ashwood-clad boxes in which all building services are enclosed.

Status
Built

Year
2014

Firm
Bernheimer Architecture

Firm location
Brooklyn, NY, USA

Awards Category **Plus** / Type **Architecture + Light** / Winner **Popular Choice**

Fondation Louis Vuitton Paris, France

As night falls, Frank Gehry's structure for the Fondation Louis Vuitton transforms from opaque shell to glowing lantern; the central core of the building begins to glow with warm white light and the glass sails, made transparent by the night sky, take on a delicate, almost diaphanous quality.

Drawing inspiration from nineteenth-century glass and garden architecture, Frank Gehry created a glass ark whose sails soar amidst the trees of the Bois de Boulogne. The twelve transparent mainsails were constructed from 3,600 glass panels and enclose a central, concrete core. Within the core are eleven galleries and a 1,000-seat modular auditorium, all dedicated to the exhibition of the Fondation Louis Vuitton's permanent collections, as well as rotating exhibitions.

As night falls, the structure is transformed from opaque shell to glowing lantern; the central core of the building begins to glow with warm white light and the glass sails, made transparent by the night sky, take on a delicate, almost diaphanous quality. The warm light from within highlights the architectural detail of both the central core and the sweeping sails wrapped around it, while never losing a sense of the structure as a single entity. The lighting gives this monumental structure buoyancy and movement, as light from the reflecting pool dapples the billowing glass sails, making the building float, ark-like, amid the green sea of trees. Dimmable, integrated LED fixtures allow for a degree of sustainability exceeding the most stringent energy policies.

Status
Built

Year
2014

Firm
L'Observatoire International

Firm location
New York, NY, USA

Awards Category **Plus** / Type **Architecture + Preservation** / Winner **Jury**

28th Street Apartments Los Angeles, CA, USA

This project includes the restoration of a historic, 24,000-square-foot YMCA building, plus a thoughtful addition that offers community programs and forty-nine supportive housing units.

The 28th Street Apartments' restoration and addition add new residential units while restoring a historic YMCA built in 1926 by architect Paul R. Williams. By 2007, the housing had been abandoned and community spaces were in disrepair. Ornament was missing, and all utilities needed to be replaced.

An interstitial floor inserted above the ground-floor ceiling hides new services, conserving the historic concrete ceilings. Lack of funds precluded fully reinstating the exterior stone coursing, and a cement coating conveys compositional intent. Nineteen code modifications were filed to preserve building integrity, enlarge existing units, and add twenty-five units. The restored 24,000-square-foot building and 15,000-square-foot addition offer community programs and forty-nine supportive housing units.

Slinging mechanical equipment between trusses over the light well avoids structurally overloading the roof deck and creates an arbor for an elevated garden, linking new and old.

To highlight the solidity of the historic building, a lightweight perforated metal screen wraps the walkways and stairs of the thin addition. Screens feather at the corners to reveal views of the city. Some perforations are tabbed rather than punctured to create a secondary pattern abstracted from the cast stone reliefs on the historic building.

Status
Built

Year
2012

Firm
Koning Eizenberg Architecture

Firm location
Santa Monica, CA, USA

Awards Category **Plus** / Type **Architecture + Preservation** / Winner **Popular Choice**

Restoration of Matrera Castle Villamartín, Spain

Carquero Arquitectura's bold restoration of a medieval stone tower in Cádiz, Spain, blends historic materiality with contemporary design.

After the partial collapse of this medieval tower, a historic landmark of the Guadalete Valley, Carquero Arquitectura designed the restoration of an icon that had lost part of its imposing volume. This project aims to restore unity without erasing the monumental traces of history.

    Therefore, the proposal avoids aesthetic mimicry that involves falsification or loss of authenticity, and uses a continuous coating similar to that of the original facade. Likewise, the upper casing enhances the original battlements, which had been hidden behind their stratigraphic superposition.

Status
Built

Year
2015

Firm
Carquero Arquitectura

Firm location
Prado del Rey, Spain

Awards Category Plus / Type Architecture + Rendering / Winner Jury

Sanguine Lily: 1916 Centenary Chapel at Glasnevin Cemetery
Dublin, Ireland

Surrounded by three reflecting pools, the modern design for a chapel honoring Ireland's 1916 Easter Rising maximizes natural and artificial light through a rounded glass curtain, an elongated skylight, and spherical lighting.

This design for a 1916 Centenary Chapel at Glasnevin Cemetery aims to unify the greater Dublin community, acting as a portal for lost loved ones and a symbol of indissoluble unity for the living.

The design seeks to build upon the rich symbolic repertoire of the nation by directly referencing the petal of an Easter Lily. Surrounded by three reflecting pools, the chapel appears from afar to be a petal floating on a puddle of water.

The main focal point of the chapel is the natural and artificial light surrounding the structure. Natural light streaming in from the north and south through the glass curtain walls enclosing the chapel, combined with 232 glass sphere lights suspended from the ceiling, allow for maximum brightness that will form a luminous crown visible in the nocturnal sky. The continuous slot that bisects the roof and acts as a skylight creates a beautiful contrast to the shadows cast after sunrise.

The Centenary Chapel aims at joining the past, present, and future in a way that takes a perfect moment and shapes it into an elegant and refined structure for all to admire.

Status
Concept

Firm
Form4 Architecture

Firm location
San Francisco, CA, USA

Awards Category **Plus** / Type **Architecture + Rendering** / Winner **Popular Choice**

Camaçari Buildings Salvador de Bahia, Brazil

Luscious visualizations for InTown Arquitetura's multi-unit housing concept in Salvador de Bahia highlight the project's strong connection with nature.

This project consists of sixty apartments facing Camaçari beach in Salvador, Bahia. The final concept for each block of apartments requires overlaying and moving six rectangles, thereby providing privacy without losing beach views. The condominium has a private club, swimming pool, restaurant, employee space, and parking spaces.

Respecting the natural environment, all native vegetation is preserved as pathways use suspended wooden decks made with native wood from Salvador. The existing trees are also preserved. The top of the building has solar panels to provide electricity, and the sides of the buildings are coated with a green wall to provide better cooling comfort: The sun in Bahia is very aggressive. The sides of the staircases have vertical wooden panels for privacy. Rainwater is used to irrigate the green walls and for sanitation.

Status
Concept

Firm
InTown Arquitetura

Firm location
**Rio de Janeiro,
Brazil**

Awards Category **Plus** / Type **Architecture + Photography & Video** / Winner **Popular Choice**

Fogo Natural Park Venue Fogo Island, Cape Verde, Portugal

Fernando Guerra captures the now destroyed PNH Headquarters amid a striking natural landscape of volcano and crater.

On Fogo Island, at an altitude of 5,900 feet, around the crater of the volcano, lies a village of about 1,200 inhabitants who live on the fringes of legality, occupying state-owned land. Agricultural activities are their means of subsistence in one of Cape Verde's poorest regions.

The natural landscape, strikingly marked by the volcano and its crater, possesses a unique and rare beauty. The idea in designing for this unusual place was to achieve a balanced solution, where architecture and landscape complement each other. The mass of the building is made of a continuous skin, composed of local black masonry block—a mixture of cement and ashes from the volcano.

During the daytime, the long walls outline the building and blend with the road, suggesting the existence of spaces through an interplay of shadows. At night, bright light is avoided as a means to protect native birds.

The challenges of a shortage of local resources became an opportunity; the building was made by the people and for the people, using local materials and techniques.

In November, 2014, seven months after the inauguration of the venue, the PNH Headquarters was destroyed in a volcanic eruption.

Status
Built

Year
2014

Firm
Fernando Guerra | FG+SG

Firm location
Lisboa, Portgal

Awards Category Plus / Type Architecture + Photography & Video / Winner Jury

House of Music Aalborg, Denmark

The House of Music employs a hybrid architecture to create a mixed-use music school and concert hall that implements porous public space to heighten creative energy.

With a typology influenced by Le Corbusier's La Tourette, the House of Music is designed as a simple yet powerful courtyard building. By wrapping the music school around the concert hall and allowing the public spaces to spill into each other, a hybrid architecture is formed.

The foyer acts as the main artery and becomes a crossing point between the space's different cultural, educational, and commercial functions. This shared energy animates the building throughout the day, allowing the potential for an exchange of ideas and knowledge between artists, educators, students, and audiences.

It is just as important to see music being played as it is to hear it. Seeing an orchestra play Beethoven's Ninth Symphony is not only exciting, it brings the emotion of music to another level. By cross-pollinating the school and concert hall, this design lets students mingle with professionals on a daily basis, making the House of Music a resonating body for creativity.

Status
Built

Year
2014

Firm
SPIRIT OF SPACE

Firm location
Chicago, IL, USA

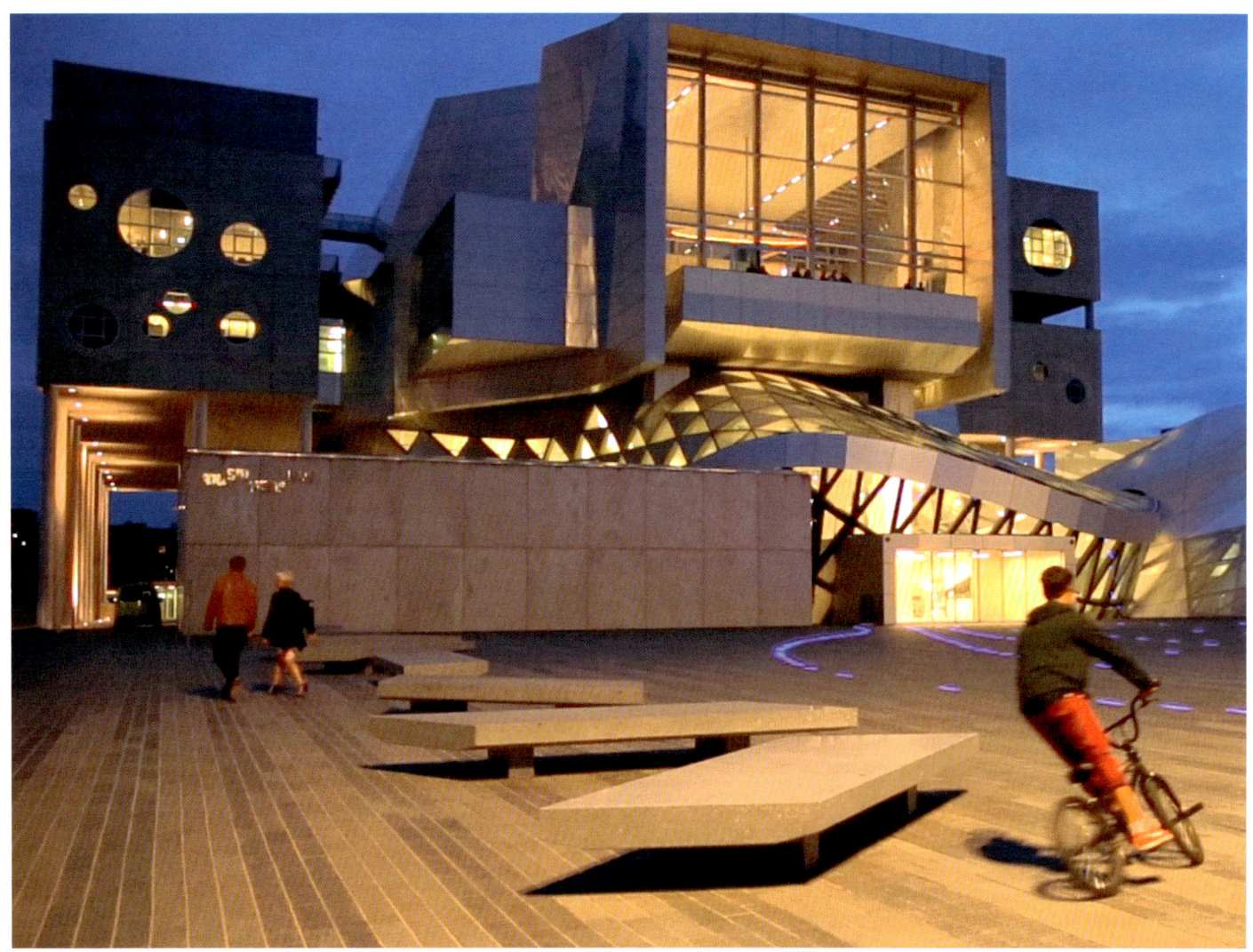

Awards Category **Plus** / Type **Architecture + Sustainability** / Winner **Popular Choice**

Helgeland Kraft's Øvre Forsland Power Station Helgeland, Norway

To complement the experience of this hydropower plant, Stein Hamre favored Kebony, a Norwegian wood produced using sustainably sourced softwood species.

Norway, a country that generates more than 80 percent of its electricity from hydropower, has added to its renewable repertoire a beautiful, Kebony-clad thirty-gigawatt-hour plant. The plant is situated deep within the mountains of Helgeland, a hiker's paradise just below the Arctic Circle. The region is known for its unique coastline and spectacular mountain formations.

Stein Hamre architects designed the sustainable hydropower plant for Helgeland Kraft to tell the story of its location and to educate about power production by allowing visitors to experience the generation of hydraulic electricity at various points throughout the process. From the nearby bridge, the powerful water flow that drives the turbines can be seen emerging from the station.

Øvre Forsland Power Station is located on the riverbank, in a clearing at the edge of a spruce forest. The verticality and irregularity of the spruce trees helped inspire the design. Along with extensive use of stone, slate, and glass on the exterior of the building, Kebony wood is used for cladding. Kebony was chosen primarily for its beauty and hardwearing qualities, but also for its sustainability. Kebony, produced using sustainable softwood, is a sustainable alternative to tropical hardwood and other modified wood.

Status
Built

Year
2015

Firm
Stein Hamre Arkitektkontor & Kebony

Firm location
Trondheim, Norway

Awards Category **Plus** / Type **Architecture + Self Initiated Projects, + Technology** / Winner **Jury & Popular Choice**

The Lowline Lab New York, NY, USA

The Lowline Lab is a 1,000-square-foot installation piece built inside an abandoned market that provides the opportunity to study plants and solar lighting in conditions that mimic the future underground Lowline community space in New York City.

The Lowline Lab is a long-term public laboratory and installation piece. Built inside an abandoned market on the Lower East Side, the Lowline Lab mimics the conditions of the future Lowline underground community space to create a variety of experiences and technical experiments.

James Ramsey, his team at Raad Studio, and the Korea-based technology company Sunportal designed and installed optical devices which capture and concentrate natural sunlight. The sunlight is sent into the warehouse through a series of tubes, directing full spectrum light into a central distribution nexus. A solar canopy then spreads out the sunlight across the space, providing light critical to sustain the plant life below.

The landscape, designed by Raad Studio and Signe Nielsen of Mathews Nielsen, is composed of over 3,000 plants and dozens of unique varieties, spread across 1,000 square feet. The Lab provides the opportunity to study plant life in the same type of environment as the future Lowline, and will help determine which types of plants will grow best underground.

Status
Built

Year
2015

Firm
Raad Studio

Firm location
New York, NY, USA

Awards Category **Plus** / Type **Architecture + Sustainability** / Winner **Jury**
Ilima Primary School Ilima, Democratic Republic of the Congo

A sustainable and innovative locally fabricated school, developed in tandem with the community, serves to promote environmental preservation in its region of the Congo jungle.

Deep in the jungle of the Congo Basin, the Ilima Primary School by MASS Design Group and the African Wildlife Foundation (AWF) sets a new standard for rural education. Built as part of AWF's strategy to encourage environmental preservation in the region, the school serves as a community center for village-level programming to promote sustainable farming and hunting practices for the mutually beneficial integration of villagers and wildlife. With its innovative design, it has become a beacon school, attracting the region's best teachers and offering students opportunities beyond subsistence farming.

Built entirely of materials and labor sourced on the hard-to-access site, the Ilima Primary School embodies MASS's ethos of Lo-Fab (local fabrication). Designers collaborated with local conservationists to identify appropriate trees in the agricultural area, which were hand-sawn, planed, and crafted into the timber trusses, roof framing, furniture, and architectural details of the final facility. Local artisans and MASS architects experimented with modified earth mixes and regional trees to form the building's walls and roof shingles.

In this way, the Ilima Primary School redefines what sustainable architecture can aspire to be. Developed in tandem with the community it serves, the rural school does not risk deteriorating with time.

Status
Built

Year
2014

Firm
MASS Design Group

Firm location
Boston, MA, USA

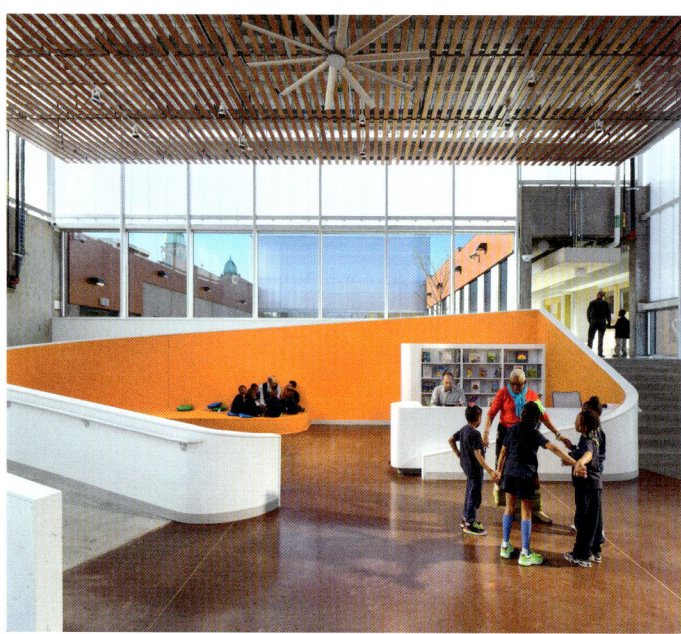

Awards Category Plus / Type Architecture + Urban Transformation / Winner Jury

Henderson-Hopkins School Baltimore, MD, USA

A sustainably built school in Baltimore is inspired by its urban context.

The new Elmer A. Henderson: A Johns Hopkins Partnership School and The Harry and Jeanette Weinberg Early Childhood Center, together called Henderson-Hopkins, is the first new Baltimore public school building in nearly thirty years. A cornerstone for the largest redevelopment project in Baltimore and a catalyst in the revitalization of East Baltimore, the seven-acre campus houses 540 students and 175 preschool children.

Inspired by a contextual interpretation of East Baltimore urban planning and by the scale and character of its row homes, the school is a composition of small scale "houses," forming larger blocks, then clusters, bisected by main streets, side streets, alleys and paths, rooting the facility in the community. Classrooms are organized into clusters by age, and the clusters center on "commons" learning spaces, spilling out onto exterior "learning terraces." The open layout and circulation provide ample sunlight inside the classrooms and encourage planned and chance interaction.

The school has become a community hub. It includes a family resource center, a library, an auditorium, and a gym. These programs are located along the neighborhood's main artery to increase community interaction. The site's history is further enhanced with the preservation and restoration of historic row homes that serve as a library for the school and the community.

The project is the first school in Baltimore to be awarded the Baltimore City Green Building Standards 3-Star certification, a LEED Gold equivalent.

Status
Built

Year
2014

Firm
ROGERS PARTNERS Architects+Urban Designers

Firm location
New York, NY, USA

Awards Category **Plus** / Type **Architecture + Urban Transformation** / Winner **Popular Choice**

The Nobel Bros Leiden, The Netherlands

The design for this modern pop venue, built on the site of a brick factory, connects with the area through a deep orange facade of Corten steel, patterned to remind visitors of the surrounding brickwork.

In order to strengthen its cultural profile and to make the city center a bigger draw, Leiden City Council decided it needed a modern pop venue. Ector Hoogstad Architecten was asked to design a striking and recognizable pop venue on a neglected nineteenth-century block in the city center. There were a number of charming houses on the block, but the real pearl was the brick factory building on the Marktsteeg.

The monumental facade on the Marktsteeg has been carefully renovated. The size and scale of the new facades are in harmony with the rhythm of the houses used to be there. The deep orange color of the Corten steel used in the new facades matches the tint of the surrounding brickwork.

The same materials are repeated on the inside: steel, brick, stone, and wood. The entrance and foyer in the old factory building are dominated by coarse, old brick facades and distinctive wooden rafters.

The highlight of the building is the main concert hall. Two U-shaped balconies give it a pleasant height and an exceptionally theatrical effect.

Status
Built

Year
2014

Firm
Ector Hoogstad Architecten

Firm location
Rotterdam, The Netherlands

Awards Category **Plus** / Type **Architecture + Workspace** / Winner **Jury**

He, She & It Erie County, NY, USA

Three distinct spaces built with purpose-specific parameters are collaged into one structure: a painting studio, an artist's workspace, and a greenhouse.

He, She & It is a collection of three distinct buildings for three spatial needs, collaged into one structure. The 1,400-square-foot building houses a work space for a painter, a ceramist/silversmith, and a greenhouse. Each space offers an atmosphere that differs radically from the others. The distinct atmospheres of the spaces reflect not only their respective uses, but also the predilections of the clients.

He is a painter. His studio is a white box. There are no windows in his work space; it is exclusively top-lit, offering even and indirect natural light, and maximizing the wall surface area for painting.

She is a ceramist and a silversmith. Her work space has dedicated areas for messy, wet ceramic work and delicate jewelry-making. Her space offers large windows with generous views and dramatic lighting.

It consists of plant life, seedlings in spring and plants in winter—clients with a very simple wish for maximum light and year-round, above-freezing temperatures. Here, a translucent polycarbonate shell, offers a zone of almost-outdoor space.

The spaces are grouped to form a cluster of three mono-pitched sheds.

Status
Built

Year
2015

Firm
Davidson Rafailidis

Firm location
Buffalo, NY, USA

Awards Category **Plus** / Type **Architecture + Workspace** / Winner **Popular Choice**

#dojowheels Kortrijk, Belgium

FIVE AM's transformable caravan provides a mobile, multifunctional space with ingenious integrated furniture for sitting, sleeping, eating, and meeting.

As a design office FIVE AM had the idea of a mobile workspace for a long time. The partners bought an old caravan and converted it into #dojowheels. The office had to be multifunctional as well as a blank canvas.

As the construction started, they explored the conversion process. Even during that process they changed details to tailor the caravan perfectly to their own needs.

They used a lightweight plywood that is more common in aviation, and covered the walls in perforated panels. Inside there is a light-emitting stretched ceiling.

The office has a couch, a bed, a meeting table for up to six people, a fridge, a storage room underneath, and storage boxes fixed to the walls. Different lighting options include reading lights, a work light above the desk, and outdoor lights.

Status
Built

Year
2015

Firm
FIVE AM

Firm location
Kortrijk, Belgium

Awards Category **Plus** / Type **Architecture + Color** / Winner **Jury**

Nanyang Primary School Singapore

An extension to a primary school in Singapore is organized around a "valley" concept of communal space, open to the sky but private at the street level; it also employs bright strips of color and shaded spaces.

The new extension to the existing Nanyang Primary School and Kindergarten in Singapore is designed around a large "valley," open to the sky but facing away from the residential streets.

When entering the valley at public street level the visitor cannot see the valley's entire extent as it curves around a strategically placed bend at its geographic center, where a large landscaped staircase is located. This landscape gesture emphasizes and enhances the existing site contours. The horizontal extent of the valley is balanced by the verticality of the stair and exposed yellow columns, on which bridges seem to fly overhead, facilitating easy connections between two parallel wings of classrooms.

Color is expressed in the form of a series of bundled horizontal stripes. Every color always appears in a group of colors, highlighting that this is a communal valley. Bundles of colors create a very different impression from individual colors, as they offer a variety of readings and interpretations. This effect is achieved through a low-cost budget application of emulsion paint on profiled, precast concrete spandrels with colored shading shelves providing protection against sun and rain.

Status
Built

Year
2015

Firm
studio505

Firm location
Melbourne, Australia

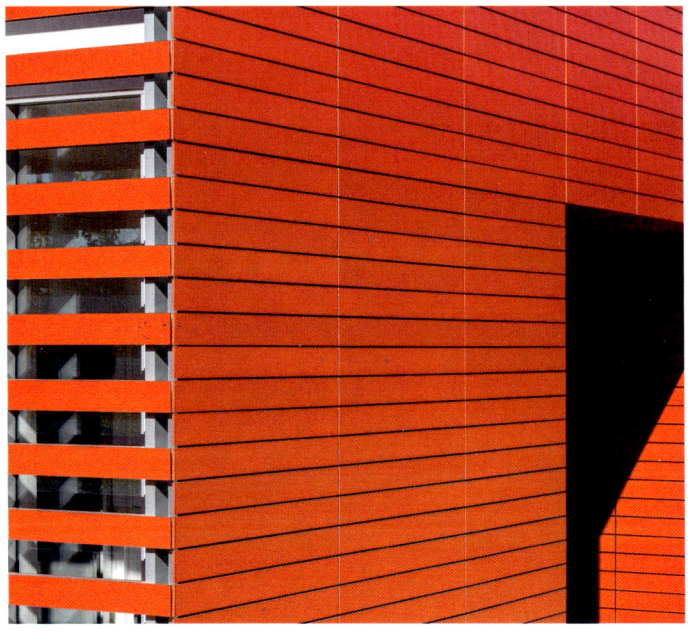

Awards Category **Plus** / Type **Architecture + Color** / Winner **Popular Choice**

Red Barn Westport, CT, USA

Roger Ferris + Partners' brilliantly bold Red Barn provides a striking contrast with the surrounding green of the Connecticut countryside.

Located on a coastal Connecticut estate, the Red Barn houses space for an artist on the first floor (a studio and workshop) as well as modern living accommodations on the second floor (a bedroom, bathroom, and living and dining areas).

In stark counterpoint to the traditionalism of the estate, the building accomplishes its functions with minimalist, graphic efficiency, reinterpreting a common New England building form. Particular attention was paid to the development of the rain-screen facade (a Swiss composite facade system), integration into the landscape, and framing views of Long Island Sound.

Status
Under Construction

Year
2015

Firm
Roger Ferris + Partners

Firm location
Westport, CT, USA

Awards Category **Plus** / Type **Architecture + 3D Printing** / Winner **Jury**

Mars Ice House Alba Mons, Mars

Mars Ice House robotically constructs a life-sustaining habitat using ice shells and a hydroponic garden in preparation for the first astronauts to arrive and live on Mars.

Scientific discoveries offer proof that bodies within our solar system are awash with water. Ice, an excellent radiation shield, safely reduces transmission of ultraviolet solar and galactic gamma rays. Mars Ice House takes advantage of water's presence on Mars and life-sustaining properties to robotically construct a habitat in advance of four astronauts who will first arrive to live on the planet's surface.

For a structure organized vertically around a lander module that houses mechanical and life support systems, multi-layered ice shells are printed within an inflated reinforced membrane. A double wall of the ice shells creates two pressurized zones: an inner insulated pressure and temperate zone containing a hydroponic garden, and an intermediate pressure-regulated zone requiring an oxygen mask. This "yard" extends the boundaries of safely occupied space and provides an overflow cavity for venting to prevent contamination.

The translucent ice shells maximize interior daylight, linking inhabitants with circadian rhythms essential to overall health. Printed in a gradient of ice thicknesses, transparent apertures offer panoramic views to the landscape.

The luminous architecture of Mars Ice House celebrates man's first presence on Mars, while embodying spatial, material, and temporal dimensions paramount to the crew's physical and psychological well-being.

Status
Under Construction

Year
2035

Firm
SEArch (Space Exploration Architecture) and Clouds AO (Clouds Architecture Office)

Firm location
New York, NY, USA

Awards Category **Plus** / Type **Architecture + 3D Printing** / Winner **Popular Choice**

AMIE 1.0 Oak Ridge, TN, USA

Skidmore, Owings & Merrill exhibits its drive to innovate with this 3D printed structure, designed to share energy with a 3D printed electric vehicle.

The Additive Manufacturing Integrated Energy (AMIE) demonstration project is a 3D-printed building designed to produce and store renewable power and to share energy wirelessly with a 3D-printed vehicle.

Through the integration of new technologies and high-performance architectural design, AMIE explores the potential of a 3D-printed panel system to condense the many functions of a conventional wall system into an integrated shell, including structure, insulation, air and moisture barriers, and exterior cladding. This could lead to zero-waste construction and reduced material consumption.

The SOM team has shown how 3D printing can allow for complex, organic geometries, optimized to reduce localized stress and mitigate turbulent exterior air flow. This structure, constructed of printed C-shape forms is post-tensioned with steel rods that reinforce the weak axis of the printed material.

The 3D-printed structure's high proportion of insulated solid surfaces (79%) to glazed areas (21%) results in an efficient energy-conserving enclosure. Flexible photovoltaic panels are integrated into the roof form and supplement the vehicle energy source. They can work in concert with a natural gas powered generator to supply energy and charge the enclosure's battery when the fixtures are not in use.

Status
Built

Year
2015

Firm
Skidmore, Owings & Merrill

Firm location
Chicago, IL, USA

Awards Category **Plus** / Type **Architecture + Humanitarianism** / Winner **Popular Choice**
Toigetation Hanoi, Vietnam

H&P Architects' toilet facilities for a school in the Cao Bang Province of Vietnam were constructed with local materials and local workers; the structure is designed to resist natural disasters

Son Lap School has a total of 485 students from kindergarten to secondary levels with more than ten classes at the main school, four branch schools, and some staff housing. None of these structures meet minimum sanitation standards.

A space that includes toilet facilities plus washing areas and vegetation was necessary. Named "toigetation," the project was designed based on three objectives: quick construction, low cost, and easy application.

Inspired by the iconic image of a large tree with a wide canopy providing shade, toigetation humbly blends into the slope at the foot of Mount Phja Da. It includes a thick layer of vegetation on its four sides and in the surrounding terraced garden. That green layer helps regulate the indoor climate, reinforce the load-bearing structure, and supply food.

Toigetation is built by local workers with local materials, with a simple construction method that anchors the structure to resist natural disasters. The project has natural ventilation and lighting.

Users can learn from the dialogue the project opens between nature and the local community. People from across the country can quickly build a toigetation by themselves within three weeks and with an estimated cost of $3,000.

Status
Built

Year
2014

Firm
H&P Architects

Firm location
Hanoi, Vietnam

Awards Category **Plus** / Type **Architecture + Prefab** / Winner **Jury**

Cà Bugnada Solduno, Switzerland

Three residential towers employ varied ceiling heights—plus a robot-assembled modular facade and brick blocks that provide a cohesive unity—linking the project to its Swiss neighborhood.

Solduno, Switzerland, is a neighborhood of eclectic, early twentieth-century bourgeois mansions and 1960s brick condos. Three buildings form an open complex that connects both sides in the neighborhood.

The towers feature one flat on each floor. Varying ceiling heights nest the flats into each other from floor to floor. Each flat features a different floor plan, creating diversified individual environments recalling the eclectic spatial variety and the atmosphere of the old townhouses.

The facades hint at the articulated interior organization of space. Thanks to the rational use of only three window types and dimensions, an expressive unity was achieved. The use of brick reinforces the link to adjacent buildings but with the help of twenty-first-century technology. In collaboration with ROB AG—an ETH spinoff responsible for digital programming—and the firm Keller AG, Buzzi studio di architettura developed a robot-assembled modular facade.

Brick blocks reminiscent of pixels form the facade's image. Their scale was chosen carefully to enable combinations adaptable to the proportions of each of the building's faces. Planned openings were cut, following a different logic, namely, the one determined by the alternation of frames and windows to fit the varied living spaces inside.

Status
Built

Year
2015

Firm
Buzzi studio di architettura

Firm location
Locarno, Switzerland

Awards Category **Plus** / Type **Architecture + Prefab** / Winner **Popular Choice**

Container Park Izmir, Turkey

Atölye Labs transformed a set of simple shipping containers into a high-tech laboratory that harnesses passive solar gain and natural ventilation to minimize its energy footprint.

The Container Park is an emerging innovation park, a part of Ege University in Izmir, Turkey. The project repurposes thirty-five secondhand shipping containers. It houses independent firms focused on biotechnology, energy, materials, and software.

Solar orientation, existing campus circulation routes, wind angles, tree-shaded areas, and the contours of the previous building helped craft a meaningful programmatic division and fluid user circulation. A vertical "beacon" container, an inner courtyard, narrow cross-circulation corridors, and ample seating spots create spaces for contemplation and refuge, as well as for spontaneous encounters and play.

The design uses passive solar strategies coupled with natural ventilation, and also enhances these systems with high insulation, solar glazing, and efficient lighting. High material reuse and recycling also reduces energy.

By placing collaborative catalysts across the site, establishing a flexible core and shell system, and designing for easy relocation, the project becomes a manifestation of a building as a prototype.

Status
Built

Year
2015

Firm
Atölye Labs

Firm location
Istanbul, Turkey

Awards Category **Plus** / Type **Architecture + Renovation** / Winner **Jury**

Tea House in Hutong Beijing, China

This project restores an aging building in Beijing and transforms it for its new use as a café, adding a curving corridor and glass walls to streamline the space while emphasizing the courtyard garden.

The building, which originally hosted company business meetings before going dormant due to poor management, is transformed into a tea café. The project design begins by analyzing the old building. Repairs in the north wing are controlled to ensure the room's historical appearance is not compromised. Repairs in the south wing aim to give the room a more modern style through a partial renovation of the roof and wall.

The new environment demands comforts the previous architecture could not sustain. For the building to be temperature resistant, it has to be completely closed. Consequently, the architects have streamlined the visual structure of the building with a flat, curvy glass corridor that creates a smooth transition from the past to the present.

The courtyard of the original architecture takes a half-inside, half-outside form, significantly increasing the beauty of the garden. The white, transparent space signifies ages of time.

Status
Built

Year
2015

Firm
Arch Studio

Firm location
Beijing, China

Awards Category **Plus** / Type **Architecture + Renovation** / Winner **Popular Choice**

Lookout Tower at Galyateto Matraszentimre, Hungary

Raw steel and concrete distinguish the reconstruction of this striking lookout tower and hikers' shelter in a mountainous region of Hungary.

The project is located near the midway point of a national tourist route that passes through northern Hungary. The lookout tower is an innovative and contextual landmark in Galyateto that will enhance the experience of the second highest peak of the Matra mountains. The materials are quite puritan, and the harmony of the stone and exposed concrete prevails in the reconstruction and extension. Together the old and new materials create a contemporary built environment.

The Galyateto lookout tower is the highest one in Hungary. Through the years trees have grown above the building's top level. That top level has now been elevated with a reinforced concrete addition. In the inner core of the extension's concrete structure three bivouac shelters are lit with colorful circular windows, creating a special atmosphere for the hikers who hanker for some rest on their journey. After this significant structural reconstruction, the retained outer wall also plays a new role. The double mass of the inner core and the encircling steel stair system is enclosed with a fine, rare woven stainless-steel mesh on the external plane of the stairs.

Status
Built

Year
2015

Firm
NARTARCHITECTS

Firm location
Budapest, Hungary

Awards Category **Typology & Plus** / Type **Hospitality: Hotels & Resorts, Architecture + Cantilever, + Glass** / Winner **Jury & Popular Choice**

Manshausen Island Resort Steigen, Norway

Holiday cabins on a Norwegian island are partially cantilevered above the sea, with floor-to-ceiling windows and panoramic views.

Manshausen Island is situated in the Steigen Archipelago off the coast of Northern Norway. The resort was planned and laid out in consideration of the island's topography and the two main existing structures: the old farmhouse and the stone quays. The old farmhouse has been carefully restored and houses a common dining area and library.

The cabins are placed on the stone quays, partially cantilevered above the sea, with one placed on a natural shelf on the rocky formations above. The positioning and orientation of all the cabins takes into consideration their individual panoramic views and privacy for the guests.

The cabins are designed to offer guests shelter and comfort while at the same time underlining the dramatic experience of the elements outside, such as the sea, landscape, changing light, weather, and seasons. Above all, the cabins endeavor to fulfill the functional requirements of the guests, with ample space for luggage and clothing/equipment, a comfortable bathroom, and a kitchen/dining area. The main bed is positioned in the main room, slightly withdrawn from the floor-to-ceiling windows, to enable the visitor an around-the-clock experience of the outside elements from a comfortable shelter.

Status
Built

Year
2015

Firm
Stinessen Arkitektur

Firm location
Tromsø, Norway

Awards Category **Plus** / Type **Architecture + Brick** / Winner **Jury**

Cloaked in Bricks Tehran, Iran

This complex facade is designed to provide privacy, moderate light, and decreased neighborhood noise, using contemporary design techniques in a very traditional Iranian material, brick.

A key characteristic of Iranian residential architecture is privacy for the residents; however, this characteristic is sometimes lost in contemporary designs.

To provide privacy yet reach other goals such as moderating light, organizing the terraces, and decreasing neighborhood noise, the architects covered the facade in a grid of openings. Brick was their top choice as it has always been used as a local building material in Iran, meeting environmental needs while creating numerous textures.

The complex form of the facade, limited construction period, and economic conditions of the project required a new construction method: eliminating mortar by punching the bricks. Parametric design software facilitated the texture design process. Despite the complex form of the facade, the construction process was easily executed by workers through simple instructions employing a system of coding.

The design was an attempt to use new techniques with an old, vernacular material, proving how traditional precedents can be revitalized to create a unique architecture.

Status
Built

Year
2015

Firm
Admun Design & Construction Studio

Firm location
Tehran, Iran

Awards Category Plus / Type Architecture + Stone / Winner Jury

Gadsby's Tavern Ice Well Alexandria, VA, USA

A rehabilitation of a historic ice well retains the original building materials and enhances exhibit space and public visibility, while addressing safety concerns and site deterioration.

Gadsby's Tavern Ice Well is nationally significant as one of the few remaining urban ice wells in the United States, and an important part of Alexandria's commercial and social history. The sidewalk area was altered to provide views into the well in the 1970s. This project focused on the preservation of the historic details of the ice well and tavern building, creating an integrated outdoor exhibit while addressing structural, storm water management, deterioration, and public safety concerns stemming from the 1970s alterations.

Rehabilitation retained all remaining historic materials, reconfigured the 1970s viewing platform, and greatly improved the visitors' experience. The integrated sidewalk features create a small amphitheater area with carved stone, didactic panels, and a subdued palette of materials. The removal of excess metal guards and brick walls enhances public safety and street visibility. The below-grade exhibit space, in curvilinear bluestone, evokes a water-eroded quarry.

An upturned concrete beam is wrapped in stone at the sidewalk level following the curve of the ice well below, and carved with key historical information. An etched-glass paver panel in the sidewalk represents the original dome-centered access opening. Lighting inside the ice well enhances visibility of the features.

Status
Built

Year
2013

Firm
BELL Architects

Firm location
Washington D.C., USA

Awards Category **Plus** / Type **Architecture + Stone** / Winner **Popular Choice**

Grand Hyatt Playa del Carmen Quintana Roo, México

Through a sophisticated selection of materials and finishes, the hotel reflects the natural context of Playa del Carmen, incorporating varied natural stones, vegetation, and water bodies.

The use of different kinds of stone played a primary role in the specification of the finishes throughout the design process for the Grand Hyatt Playa del Carmen. The principal aim was achieved with the application of different sizes, colors, and textures that generate a wide array of sensations in response to the interior, exterior, and transitional spaces.

One of the most striking points in the hotel is the cenote in the spa area, a typical feature of the natural surroundings. This cenote, clad in dark gray slate, appears to emerge from the ground above El Paseo, an open-air covered pedestrian walkway that provides a stepped transition from the entrance to the shore.

Another space where natural stone plays a leading role is the imposing Maya-inspired staircase that both receives guests from the motor lobby and provides access to the ballroom. Miracema granite was used both for the floor and the fountain.

The selection of materials and finishes reflects an effort to adapt the building to the context, using sand-colored cladding, local limestone, natural wood, and incorporating vegetation and water bodies.

Status
Built

Year
2015

Firm
Sordo Madaleno

Firm location
Mexico City, Mexico

Awards Category **Plus** / Type **Architecture + Concrete** / Winner **Popular Choice**
Ma Vie La — Selim Erdil Çeşme, Turkey

The striking cantilevered form of this private residence in Turkey celebrates the material contrast between board formed concrete and rich timber shutters.

This project is a house with a strict minimalist approach. Half of the visible structure is cantilevered and the superstructure is a twenty-five-foot-wide concrete box with no columns or beams. The land, only 5,600 square feet in area, contains this very large three-story house with only a 650-square-foot footprint. The rest of the house is all terraces, a large garden, and a semi-Olympic-size pool. The cantilever was designed to minimize the footprint of the house and maximize the garden area, while pushing the building mass toward the sea view and clearing the neighboring houses. Additionally, the cantilever serves to create plenty of shade by the poolside.

The steep grade of the lot would have created unusably, long and narrow side gardens terminated by very tall retaining walls. So it was decided to use the building's side facade and the property border retaining wall as a pool basin, connecting the two at the end with an L-shaped concrete wall. This not only allowed for a very large pool but also a large garden.

The landscaping uses mostly indigenous plants in Corten-steel-clad concrete planters. The gardens are watered with rainwater collected year-round in a cistern.

Status
Built

Year
2015

Firm
Erdil Insaat

Firm location
Izmir, Turkey

Awards Category **Plus** / Type **Architecture + Metal** / Winner **Jury & Popular Choice**

City View Garage Miami, FL, USA

A parking garage in Miami sports a facade composed of curvilinear shapes, punched and bent out of titanium-coated stainless steel, allowing for natural light and ventilation with a unique and iconic aesthetic.

The prominent location of the site on the periphery of its neighborhood and its adjacency to the I-195 freeway mark this building as a landmark in the Design District in Miami. From the freeway, the facade appears as a shimmering mirage. At street level, folded fins generate textures that echo the forms of surrounding palms.

    Like Gerhard Richter's photo paintings, this facade both reflects and dissolves into the environment. The variegated pattern absorbs the qualities of the environment and disrupts the legibility of the form. From inside the garage, the wave-like shapes of the openings create a patterned view of the city. This kind of baroque minimalism blurs figure, texture, and materiality into a camouflaged icon.

    The surface is composed of curvilinear shapes, punched and bent out of gold-tinted, titanium-coated stainless steel. The openings in the facade are required to maintain natural light and ventilation in the parking structure, but the pattern of the openings transforms this functional requirement into an iconic urban object.

Status
Built

Year
2014

Firm
LEONG LEONG

Firm location
New York, NY, USA

Awards Category **Plus** / Type **Architecture + Wood** / Winner **Popular Choice**

Harbin Opera House Harbin, China

The Harbin Opera House feels like an extension of the Songhua River with a series of undulating lines that integrate the sinuous landscape into a formal building mass.

The Harbin Opera House is located on land reclaimed from the north side of the Songhua River's floodplain, providing an important locus for Harbin's rapidly expanding metropolis. Inscribed in the flat plains of the surrounding landscape, meandering patterns reveal a flowing history—they document time. Through its dynamic landscape qualities, the Songhua River contributes to Harbin's cultural, economic, and spiritual identity.

In response to nature's force and spirit, Harbin Opera House is an extension of the river with a series of undulating lines that integrate the sinuous landscape into a formal building mass. The facade reveals hidden paths that provide access for entry and viewing platforms. Clad by pillowed aluminum panels on the exterior, the snowdrift form continues into the white interior, conceptually sculpted by wind and water.

Clad in a warm wood veneer, the main theater's interior emulates a single wooden block gently eroded by natural forces to reveal layers of growth.

In fact, the construction of these elements relied on highly controlled digital fabrication techniques and an intensive handcrafted approach. Glass Fiber Reinforced Plastic (GFRP) panels were milled by computer-controlled fabrication machines to provide the geometric base on which multiple layers of wood veneer were laid and finished.

Status
Built

Year
2015

Firm
MAD Architects

Firm location
Santa Monica, CA, USA

Awards Category **Plus** / Type **Architecture + Facades** / Winner **Jury**

242 State Street Los Altos, CA, USA

This adaptive re-use project replaces the front facade with a double-height window wall that can be raised or lowered and also employs a flexible open-plan design plus skylights for added natural light.

Located in downtown Los Altos, California, this adaptive re-use project introduces a dynamic new facade that enables the 1950s building to morph from an enclosed structure into an environment that invites the community into the space. The transformation was achieved by replacing the entire front facade with a double-height, single-hung window wall that can be raised or lowered via a custom-designed hand-cranked gizmo.

The gizmo is operated by engaging a pedal which unlocks the safety mechanism, and then turning a hand wheel to activate a series of gears and pulleys that opens the sixteen-foot by ten-foot, 2,000-pound window wall. When closed, visitors enter through a ten-foot-tall custom steel pivot door. In addition to the front facade, other building modifications include raising the roof a half story to create a better proportioned interior volume, and installing skylights to bring in more natural light.

Beyond the application of kinetic architecture, custom detailing, and increased height of the primary space, the open-plan design allows the space to remain as flexible as possible for future tenants.

Status
Built

Year
2014

Firm
Olson Kundig

Firm location
Seattle, WA, USA

Awards Category **Plus** / Type **Architecture + Facades** / Winner **Popular Choice**

BCM Headquarters Ballarat, Australia

The elegant design and refined materiality of the BCM Headquarters are represented through the punctuated facade by a crosshatch of glazing, concrete, and Corten-steel accents.

The Ballarat Construction Management (BCM) Headquarters sits in a peri-urban industrial zone of a thriving regional metropolis. The elegant design pushes the boundaries of construction and form, while employing a refined material and patterning language to unify the project.

This language is represented through the punctuated facade by a crosshatch of glazing, concrete, and Corten-steel accents.

Tensions between the design intent and functional constraints were overcome through creative design-build solutions between architect and client, such as the silicon glass panels rebated into concrete frames without channels or framing, pushing sheet size beyond conventional measures. Another solution is the diagonal concrete band beams interconnecting through corners and the top of the structure.

Continuing the language of the external facade, the light-filled double-height entrance foyer features a suspended triple pendant and polished concrete cantilevered staircase. To the rear a slatted timber screen softens the space visually and acoustically, concealing storage, a workshop, staff amenities, and access to the warehouse. Upstairs a generous director's office, boardroom, and a combination of cellular and open-plan office space promote a creative, flexible workplace.

Status
Built

Year
2015

Firm
Crosier Scott Architects

Firm location
Hawthorn, Australia

Awards Category **Plus** / Type **Architecture + Ceilings** / Winner **Jury**
Delft Station Hall Delft, The Netherlands

A newly designed train station with airy spaces and vaulted ceilings hints at the city of Delft's craft history.

The newly designed station will allow travelers to experience Delft as a city not only of rich history but also of technological ingenuity. The vaulted ceilings, with scenes depicted in delft blue, create an organic blanket that covers the station and the city hall. These ceilings can be seen anywhere in the building and highlight the craft history of the city in a contemporary manner.

Status
Built

Year
2015

Firm
Mecanoo

Firm location
Delft, The Netherlands

Awards Category **Plus** / Type **Architecture + Ceilings** / Winner **Popular Choice**

CHOCOBEN Tehran, Iran

A fractal composition of multicolored elements adorns the ceiling of this cake shop in the Iranian capital of Tehran.

CHOCOBEN is one of the most famous brands of cakes and cupcakes in Iran. The shop has an area of 365 square feet and is located on one of the most crowded streets in Tehran. The design of the project began in late October 2015 and construction began at the beginning of January 2016.

One of the main issues was creating visual variation in a small space. The use of color, including light pink, gray, and white, as well as the arrangement and composition of the interior, combined with various lighting, creates a pleasant and specific atmosphere.

In the end, what is eye-catching is the use of more than 400 different-sized pieces as a parametric volume hanging from the ceiling alongside Plexiglas light volumes.

Status
Under Construction

Year
2016

Firm
AKAD Design Group

Firm location
Tehran, Iran

Awards Category **Plus** / Type **Architecture + Stairs** / Winner **Jury**

Upper East Side Duplex Stair New York, NY, USA

A duplex apartment in Manhattan is renovated into a streamlined space with a bold stair made of folded perforated steel.

The client's eclectic and sophisticated collection of museum quality art and furniture drove the initial design discussions for the gut architectural renovation and interior design of a duplex apartment on the Upper East Side of Manhattan. SPAN strove to create a gallery setting with residential detailing and warmth, a modern and equally sophisticated backdrop for these freestanding elements. This was accomplished by ensuring that spaces were seamlessly connected, that material application was sublime, and that the details were taut and rigorously simple.

Rooms connect with overscaled openings and door panels so that spaces flow together and remain undefined and scaleless. There is a necessary abundance of clutter-reducing hidden storage to achieve clean extended walls throughout the apartment. Carefully integrated lighting recalls both gallery quality and an art conceit in itself, so that when an art piece is removed, the textural wall surfaces and spatial shapes made from the walls and coves become the item of contemplation.

The other primary design consideration was the central space where the connecting stair emerges between the two floors. Occupied by a transparent stair made of folded perforated steel buffered by fumed oak wall paneling, this vertical space organizes the other programs around it, and creates a dramatic focal point.

Status
Built

Year
2015

Firm
SPAN Architecture

Firm location
New York, NY, USA

Awards Category **Plus** / Type **Architecture + Stairs** / Winner **Popular Choice**

Essex University Silberrad Student Centre Colchester, UK

Patel Taylor's ribbons of dark steel and rich timber ascend the atrium at the heart of the University of Essex's new student center in the United Kingdom.

Designed and built in tune with an extension to the Albert Sloman library, the new Silberrad Student Centre and lakeside square have created an important new front door to the University of Essex's Colchester campus. As the largest new building on the campus since 1965, the center provides an integrated learning center, a student media center, and a boardroom for the University Council.

During the development of the Student Centre, a key tenet of Patel Taylor's design was to deliver a robust frame in which the university could house an evolving program of uses without compromising the integrity of the building. The building is composed of stacked, cantilevered concrete floor slabs held apart by stone piers. Where these slabs slip apart, large volumes are created, including the three-story atrium at the heart of the building into which the welded steel staircase springs.

Appearing as continuous flowing forms of plate steel, this sculptural staircase moves vertically and horizontally like falling ribbons. From its central location, the staircase has views to the library and to the lake. Cloverleaf section oak handrails complete the composition, the material seeming warm to the touch in contrast with the cold steel and concrete.

Status
Built

Year
2015

Firm
Patel Taylor

Firm location
London, UK

Awards Category **Plus** / Type **Architecture + Water** / Winner **Jury**

Casa Meztitla Tepoztlan, Mexico

An unobtrusive stone house is designed to maximize outdoor space and rain water.

Casa Meztitla showcases the luxurious value of leisure, the tropical weather, the intense sunlight, the smells of nature, the 500-year-old surrounding landscaped terraces, and the ever-present rock mountain of El Tepozteco. The house, built out of rough stone, lies low under the trees, aligned with the stone slopes. Only two elements reveal the project's existence to the outside world: the colorful bougainvillea flowers showing randomly through the trees' dense foliage, marking the plot's perimeter; and the massive, monolithic white box that emerges through the treetops.

The house's theme is the never-ending relationship between the indoors and outdoors. There is no way one can go from one area to another without walking through outdoor spaces; every area (except for services) is open to the exterior.

Two main storm water reservoirs exist: the potable water reservoir which is covered by the grass patio, and the maintenance water reservoir, which is circular and open to the environment. The system provides enough water for the house all year round. Ideally, this storm water management plan captures every drop of rain that touches the property and uses it in different ways.

Status
Built

Year
2014

Firm
EDAA

Firm location
Mexico City, Mexico

Awards Category **Plus** / Type **Architecture + Water** / Winner **Popular Choice**

Casa Bahia Miami, FL, USA

Alejandro Landes's beautiful Casa Bahia is an exhibition in lightness, hovering over ground and water in southern Florida.

Casa Bahia is a modernist structure that seamlessly cohabits with the tropical wonderland of Coconut Grove. It appears to float above water and lush greenery, seeming to blur the boundaries between indoor and outdoor living. This is a dwelling that effortlessly merges the experience of urban living with a philosophy of simplicity, timelessness, and light.

One becomes enveloped by a home that fully absorbs every sense. The view extends infinitely into the horizon, giving the feeling of vastness. A two-story water-wall cascades with rhythmic force against smooth stones.

A suspended staircase seems to effortlessly glide over air and water, appearing to defy the pressure of gravity. A central area is uninterrupted by material divisions. In this cultivated wild, a transparent ribbon of floor-to-ceiling glass doors slide open to invite the moon, stars, and sun to inhabit this space. Excellence lies in the quality of the natural materials, the geometric sensibility, and the spirit of modernity that evokes the aesthetics of Le Corbusier merged with an eternal dreamscape unique to Miami.

Status
Built

Year
2015

Firm
Alejandro Landes

Firm location
Miami, FL, USA

Index

Page numbers in **bold** refer to illustrations

A
Adidas Boston Marathon Runbase 155 **155**
Admun Design & Construction Studio, Cloaked in Bricks 214 **215** 215
The Afsharians' House 32 33 **33**
Agag+Paredes, Valdemonjas Winery 66 67 **67**
AGATHOM, Rainforest Retreat 16 17 **17**
AKAD Design Group, CHOCOBEN 230 **230**
Alpine Shelter – A Room With a View 152 153 **153**
AMIE 1.0 201 **201**
The ANTI-KIOSK 60 61 **61**
Anti-Museum 89 **89**
Apple Store – Stanford 52 53 **53**
APRT (Arkkiteht-ityöhuone Artto Palo Rossi Tikka Architects), Rovaniemi Sports Arena 82 83 **83**
Arch Studio, Tea House in Hutong 208 209 **209**
Architectural Services Department, Crematorium in Wo Hop Shek 124 125 **125**
Architecture Workshop PC, Pivot 10 11 **11**
Arckit 169 **169**
ATLAS Tiny House 163 **163**
Atölye Labs, Container Park 206 207 **207**
Autoban, Heydar Aliyev International Airport 134 135 **135**

B
bandesign, Mirrors 72 73 **73**
Barangaroo Reserve 126 **126**
Bathaei, Ahmad, TERMEH Office – Retail Building 44 45 **45**
BCM Headquarters 226 227 **227**
Beale Street Landing 141 **143**
BELL Architects, Gadsby's Tavern Ice Well 216 **216**
Bernheimer Architecture, Quonochontaug Residence 172 173 **173**
The Bicycle Bridge Across the Sava River 144 145 **145**
Biesbosch MuseumEiland 90 91 **91**
Black Ocean Firehouse 62 63 **63**
Bohlin Cywinski Jackson, Apple Store – Stanford 52 53 **53**
Boombox Micro Retail 59 **59**
Buttress, Wolfgang, UK Pavilion – Milan Expo 2015 106 **106**
Buzzi studio di architettura, Cà Bugnada 204 205 **205**

C
Cà Bugnada 204 205 **205**
Camaçari Buildings 179 **179**
CannonDesign, Centre Hospitalier de l'Université de Montréal 81 **81**
CaoPu studio, Humble Hostel 162 **162**
Cárdenas, Rafael de, Black Ocean Firehouse 62 63 **63**
Carquero Arquitectura, Restoration of Matrera Castle 177 **177**
Casa Bahia 236 237 **237**
Casa Candelaria 20 21 **21**
Casa Meztlila 234 235 **235**
Centre Hospitalier de l'Université de Montréal 81 **81**
Cetra Ruddy, The Choice School 123 **123**
CHANG Architects, Cornwall Gardens 26 26 **27**
Charles Smith Wines Jet City 76 **76**
Cherem, arqs, Casa Candelaria 20 21 **21**
Chesapeake Car Park 4 138 139 **139**
Chinese University of Hong Kong, School of Architecture, ZCB Bamboo Pavilion 166 167 **167**
CHOCOBEN 230 **230**
The Choice School 123 **123**
Choy House 22 23 **23**
City View Garage 220 221 **221**
Cloaked in Bricks 214 215 **215**
Clouds AO (Clouds Architecture Office), Mars Ice House 200 **200**
COEX 55 **55**
Colorado Building Workshop, Colorado Outward Bound School Micro Cabins 14 15 **15**
Colorado Outward Bound School Micro Cabins 14 15 **15**
Container Park 206 207 **207**
Corner (James) Field Operations, Philadelphia Navy Yards Central Green 127 **127**
Cornwall Gardens 26 26 **27**
Crematorium Hofheide 102 103 **103**
Crematorium in Wo Hop Shek 124 125 **125**
Crosier Scott Architects, BCM Headquarters 226 227 **227**
CrystalZoo, Expansion of Government Offices 107 **107**
CTAA Architecture Lab 96 97 **97**
Culture House and Library 118 119 **119**

D
dans arhitekti, The Bicycle Bridge Across the Sava River 144 145 **145**
Davidson Rafailidis, He, She & It 192 193 **193**
Davis (Sharon) Design, Doctors' Housing for Partners in Health 160 161 **161**
Delft Station Hall 228 229 **229**
Destination Spa + Resort 80 **80**
Diamond Schmitt Architects/ Siavash Vazirnezami, Intern Architect, Anti-Museum 89 **89**
Dioinno Architecture, High Living 42 **42**
Doctors' Housing for Partners in Health 160 161 **161**
#dojowheels 194 195 **195**
Dokk1 120 121 **121**
DUBBELDAM Architecture + Design, Skygarden House 40 41 **41**

E
Ector Hoogstad Architecten, The Nobel Bros 190 191 **191**
EDAA, Casa Meztlila 234 235 **235**
Elliott + Associates, Chesapeake Car Park 4 138 139 **139**
Ennead Architects, Rethinking Refugee Communities 130 **130**
Erdil Insaat, Ma Vie La – Selim Erdil 218 219 **219**
Essex University Silberrad Student Centre 232 233 **233**
Expansion of Government Offices 107 **107**

F
F9 Productions Inc, ATLAS Tiny House 163 **163**
Ferris (Roger) + Partners, Red Barn 198 199 **199**
Field Operations, Philadelphia Navy Yards Central Green 127 **127**
FIVE AM, #dojowheels 194 195 **195**
Flamingo Shanghai Office – The Attic 64 65 **65**
Fogo Island Artist Studios 150 151 **151**
Fogo Natural Park Venue 180 181 **181**
Fondation Louis Vuitton 174 175 **175**
Fontaine/Fortin/Labelle, Petite Vie 168 **168**
Forestaurant 74 75 **75**
Form4 Architecture, Sanguine Lily: 1916 Centenary Chapel at Glasnevin Cemetery 178 **178**

G
Gadsby's Tavern Ice Well 216 **216**
Gensler, COEX 55 **55**
GM Architectes Associés, Meditation Pavilion & Garden 128 129 **129**
Golden Ratio 43 **43**
Govaert & Vanhoutte Architectuurburo, Golden Ratio 43 **43**
Grace Farms 164 165 **165**
Grand Hyatt Playa Del Carmen 217 **217**
Great Amber – Concert Hall 100 101 **101**
The Great Wall of WA (The Musterers' Quarters) 30 31 **31**
Greatrex (Tim) Architect, House of Vans London 68 **68**
The Greja House 24 25 **25**
Guerra (Fernando) | FG+SG, Fogo Natural Park Venue 180 181 **181**
Guessing Agriculture School 114 115 **115**

H
H&P Architects
 Forestaurant 74 75 **75**
 Toigetation 202 203 **203**
Hadid (Zaha) Architects, Messner Mountain Museum Corones 92 93 **93**
Hamad International Airport 136 137 **137**
Hanazono Kindergarten and Nursery 108 109 **109**
Handel Architects, 170 Amsterdam 36 37 **37**
Harbin Opera House 222 223 **223**
He, She & It 192 193 **193**
Henderson-Hopkins School 188 189 **189**
Henriquez Partners Architects, TELUS Garden Office Tower 54 **54**
Heydar Aliyev International Airport 134 135 **135**
HIBINOSEKKEI + Youji no Shiro, Hanazono Kindergarten and Nursery 108 109 **109**
High Living 42 **42**
Highpark 34 **34**
HOK, Hamad International Airport 136 137 **137**
House of Music 182 **182**
House of Vans London 68 **68**
Humble Hostel 162 **162**

I
Ilima Primary School 186 187 **187**
InTown Arquitetura, Camaçari Buildings 179 **179**

J
Jaklitsch/Gardner Architects, Mizengo Pinda Asali & Nyuki Sanctuary – Beekeeping & Education Center 122 **122**
Jerry House 38 39 **39**
JTI Headquarters 50 51 **51**

K
The Kindergarten of the German School of Athens 110 111 **111**
Koning Eizenberg Architecture, 28th Street Apartments 176 **176**
KOUROSH RAFIEY Architectural Design Studio (KRDS), Sohanak Swimming Pool 86 87 **87**
Kurve 7 56 57 **57**

L
LaGuardia Airport Master Plan 149 **149**
Landes, Alejandro, Casa Bahia 236 237 **237**
Latent Design, Boombox Micro Retail 59 **59**
Law Architects, Woodleigh School – Homestead Project 170 171 **171**
LEONG LEONG, City View Garage 220 221 **221**
Ley (Rob) Studio, May–September 140 **140**
L'Observatoire International, Fondation Louis Vuitton 174 175 **175**
Lookout Tower at Galyateto 210 211 **211**
The Lowline Lab 184 185 **185**

M
Ma Vie La – Selim Erdil 218 219 **219**
MAD Architects, Harbin Opera House 222 223 **223**
Manshausen Island Resort 212 213 **213**
Marman-Borins-Khamsi, SFC Bridge 146 147 **147**
Mars Ice House 200 **200**
MASS Design Group, Ilima Primary School 186 187 **187**
May–September 140 **140**
Mecanoo, Delft Station Hall 228 229 **229**
Meditation Pavilion & Garden 128 129 **129**
Mehdizadeh, Farshad, TERMEH Office – Retail Building 44 45 **45**
Messner Mountain Museum Corones

92 93 **93**
MIA Design Studio, Naman Retreat Pure Spa 76 77 **77**
Michaelis Boyd, Sandibe Safari Lodge 70 71 **71**
Mirrors 72 73 **73**
Mizengo Pinda Asali & Nyuki Sanctuary — Beekeeping & Education Center 122 **122**
Mori (Toshiko) Architect, Thread: Artists' Residency and Cultural Center **158** 159 **159**

N
Nakamura (Hiroshi) & NAP, Sayama Forest Chapel 104 105 **105**
Naman Retreat Pure Spa 78 79 **79**
Nanyang Primary School **196** 197 **197**
NARTARCHITECTS, Lookout Tower at Galyateto 210 211 **211**
Nathalie Mauclair Gymnasium **84** 85 **85**
National Design Centre 94 95 **95**
Neri & Hu, Flamingo Shanghai Office — The Attic **64** 65 **65**
NEUF Architect(e)s, Centre Hospitalier de l'Université de Montréal 81 **81**
Nevern Square Apartment 12 13 **13**
New Wave Architecture, Polur Rock Gym 88 **88**
The Nobel Bros **190** 191 **191**

O
Ocean Breeze Track and Field House 82 **82**
odD+, the ANTI-KIOSK 60 61 **61**
Odin Bar + Café 77 **77**
OfficeAT, PTTEP-S1 Office 46 47 **47**
Olson Kundig
  Charles Smith Wines Jet City 76 **76**
  Shinsegae International 46 47 **47**
  242 State Street **224** 225 **225**
  170 Amsterdam 36 37 **37**
O'Neill Rose Architects, Choy House 22 23 **23**
OneOcean Marina Port Vell **142** 143 **143**
onion, Jerry House 38 39 **39**
Oppenheim Architecture, Destination Spa + Resort 80 **80**
OVD 919 28 29 **29**

P
Parc Office, Adidas Boston Marathon Runbase 155 **155**
Park + Associates, The Greja House 24 25 **25**
Patel Taylor, Essex University Silberrad Student Centre **232** 233 **233**
People's Architecture Office, Tubular Baitasi 157 **157**
Petite Vie 168 **168**
Petteno (Daniele) Architecture Workshop, Nevern Square Apartment 12 13 **13**
Phaedrus Studio, Odin Bar + Café 77 **77**
Philadelphia Navy Yards Central Green 127 **127**
Pichler & Traupmann Architekten, Guessing Agriculture School **114** 115 **115**

Pivot 10 11 **11**
Polur Rock Gym 88 **88**
Potiropoulos + Partners, The Kindergarten of the German School of Athens 110 111 **111**
Primus Arkitekter, Culture House and Library 118 119 **119**
P.S. 62 The Kathleen Grimm School for Leadership and Sustainability 112 113 **113**
PTTEP-S1 Office 46 47 **47**
Puri (Sanjay) Architects, Reservoir 69 **69**
PWP Landscape Architecture, Barangaroo Reserve 126 **126**

Q
Quonochontaug Residence **172** 173 **173**

R
Raad Studio, The Lowline Lab **184** 185 **185**
Rainforest Retreat 16 17 **17**
RCR Arquitectes, Crematorium Hofheide 102 103 **103**
Red Barn 198 199 **199**
ReNa Design, The Afsharians' House 32 33 **33**
Reservoir 69 **69**
Restoration of Matrera Castle 177 **177**
Rethinking Refugee Communities 130 **130**
Rieder Smart Elements, Alpine Shelter — A Room With a View **152** 153 **153**
ROGERS PARTNERS Architects+Urban Designers, Henderson-Hopkins School **188** 189 **189**
Rojkind Arquitectos, Highpark 34 **34**
Rosselli (Luigi) Architects, The Great Wall of WA (The Musterers' Quarters) 30 31 **31**
RTN, Beale Street Landing 141 **141**

S
Sage and Coombe Architects, Ocean Breeze Track and Field House 82 **82**
Sandibe Safari Lodge 70 71 **71**
Sanguine Lily: 1916 Centenary Chapel at Glasnevin Cemetery 178 **178**
SAOTA, OVD 919 28 29 **29**
Saunders Architecture, Fogo Island Artist Studios 150 151 **151**
Sayama Forest Chapel 104 105 **105**
SCDA Architects Singapore
  National Design Centre 94 95 **95**
  SkyTerrace@Dawson 35 **35**
SCHEMAA, Nathalie Mauclair Gymnasium **84** 85 **85**
schmidt hammer lassen architects, Dokk1 120 121 **121**
School of Architecture — Royal Institute of Technology 116 117 **117**
SCOB Architecture & Landscape, OneOcean Marina Port Vell **142** 143 **143**
SEArch (Space Exploration Architecture), Mars Ice House 200 **200**
SFC Bridge 146 147 **147**
The Shakespearean Theatre 98 99 **99**

Shinsegae International 48 49 **49**
SHoP Architects
  LaGuardia Airport Master Plan 149 **149**
  TalkBox 156 **156**
Silman (Robert) Associates, Grace Farms 164 165 **165**
Skidmore, Owings & Merrill
  AMIE 1.0 201 **201**
  JTI Headquarters 50 51 **51**
  P.S. 62 The Kathleen Grimm School for Leadership and Sustainability 112 113 **113**
  The Strand — Environmental Graphics 154 **154**
Skygarden House 40 41 **41**
SkyTerrace@Dawson 35 **35**
Sohanak Swimming Pool 86 87 **87**
SOMA, Unilux 56 **56**
SPAN Architecture, Upper East Side Duplex Stair 231 **231**
SPIRIT OF SPACE, House of Music 182 **182**
Stein Hamre Arkitektkontor & Kebony, Helgeland Kraft's Øvre Forsland Power Station 183 **183**
Stinessen Arkitektur, Manshausen Island Resort 212 213 **213**
The Strand — Environmental Graphics 154 **154**
studio505, Nanyang Primary School **196** 197 **197**
Studio Marco Vermeulen, Biesbosch MuseumEiland 90 91 **91**
studio PROTOTYPE, Villa Schoorl **18** 19 **19**
stu/D/O Architects, Kurve 7 **56** 57 **57**
Sutton, Alex, Stockholm Airport City 148 **148**

T
Tabanlioglu Architects, Yenikapi Transfer Point and Archaeo-Park Area 131 **131**
TalkBox 156 **156**
Tea House in Hutong 208 209 **209**
TELUS Garden Office Tower 54 **54**
TERMEH Office — Retail Building 44 45 **45**
Tham & Videgård Arkitekter, School of Architecture — Royal Institute of Technology 116 117 **117**
Thread: Artists' Residency and Cultural Center **158** 159 **159**
Toigetation 202 203 **203**
Tubular Baitasi 157 **157**
28th Street Apartments 176 **176**
242 State Street **224** 225 **225**

U
UK Pavilion — Milan Expo 2015 106 **106**
Unilux 58 **58**
University of Colorado Denver, Colorado Outward Bound School Micro Cabins 14 15 **15**
UNStudio, Arnhem Central Master Plan 134 135 **135**
Upper East Side Duplex Stair 231 **231**

V
Valdemonjas Winery 66 67 **67**
Vandersanden Group, The Shakespearean Theatre 98 99 **99**

Villa Schoorl **18** 19 **19**
Volker Giencke & Company, Great Amber — Concert Hall **100** 101 **101**

W
Woodleigh School — Homestead Project 170 171 **171**

Y
Yenikapi Transfer Point and Archaeo-Park Area 131 **131**

Z
ZCB Bamboo Pavilion 166 167 **167**

Acknowledgments

This book is dedicated to the world's architects.

Thank you to the Architizer team, with a special thanks to Nikki-Lee Birdsey, Joanna Kloppenburg, Chloé Vadot, and Nicole Tetreault.

Phaidon Press Limited
Regent's Wharf
All Saints Street
London N1 9PA

Phaidon Press Inc.
65 Bleecker Street
New York, NY 10012

phaidon.com

First published 2016
© 2016 Phaidon Press Limited

ISBN 978 0 7148 7287 2

A CIP catalogue record for this book is available from the British Library and the Library of Congress.

All rights reserved. No part of this publication may be reproduced, stored in a retrieval system, or transmitted, in any form or by any means, electronic, mechanical, photocopying, recording or otherwise, without the written permission of Phaidon Press Limited.

Commissioning Editor: Emilia Terragni
Project Editor: Laura Loesch-Quintin
Production Controllers: Nerissa Vales, Sue Medlicott
Design: Aaron Garza

The publisher would like to thank Sophie Fels and Vanessa Bird for their contributions to the book.

Printed in U.S.A.

Photography Credits

Every reasonable effort has been made to acknowledge the ownership of copyright for photographs included in this volume. Any errors that may have occurred are inadvertent and will be corrected in subsequent editions, provided notification is sent in writing to the publisher.

Robert Garneau: 10-11; Daniele Petteno Architecture Workshop: 12-13; Jesse Kuroiwa: 14-15; Steven Evans: 16-17; Jeroen Musch: 18-19; Enrique Macías: 20-21; Clouds AO + SEArch: 22-23; Edward Hendricks: 24-25; Albert Lim K.S.: 26-27; Adam Letch: 28-29; Justin Alexander & Edward Birch: 30-31; Reza Najafian/Hossein Hamzelouei: 32-33; Courtesy of Rojkind Arquitectos; Photo by Jaime Navarro: 34; Aaron Polock: 35; Bruce Damonte: 36-37; Wison Tungthunya W Workspace: 38-39; Shai Gil, Studio Shai Gil: 40-41; Jin Young Song: 42; Govaert & Vanhoutte Architects: 43; Parham Taghiof: 44-45; Wison Tungthunya: 46-47; Kyungsub Shin Studio/Olson Kundig: 48-49; Hufton+Crow: 50 (cl, cr, bl, br); Adrien Barakat©JTI: 50 (tl, tr), 51; Peter Aaron: 52 (tr, bl); Hufton+Crow: 52 (tl, c, br), 53; Ed White: 54; Nacása & Partners: 55; Ketsiree Wongwan: 56-57; SOMA: 58; Latent Design: 59; Enrique Aviles: 60-61; Floto+Warner/OTTO: 62-63; Dirk Weiblen: 64-65; Carlos Jiménez: 66-67; Tim Greatrex: 68; Sanjay Puri Architects: 69; DOOK: 70-71; Shigetomo Mizuno: 72-73; Doan Thanh Ha: 74-75; Kevin Scott/Olson Kundig: 76; Ryan Fung Photography: 77; Hiroyuki Oki: 78-79; Luxigon: 80; CannonDesign and NEUF Architect(e)s: 81; Paul Warchol: 82; Aaro Artto: 83; David Foessel: 84-85; kourosh rafiey: 86-87; New Wave Architecture (Lida Almassian/Shahin Heidari): 88; Anti-Museum: 89; Ronald Tilleman: 90-91; Hufton+Crow: 92 (t, bl, br); inexhibit: 92 (cl); Werner Huthmacher: 92 (cr); Werner Huthmacher: 93; Aaron Polock: 94-95; Cha Shao Yu: 96-97; Rafał Malko: 98-99; Indrikis Sturmanis, Riga/Latvia: 100-101; hisao suzuki: 102-103; Hiroshi Nakamura & NAP Co., Ltd.: 104-105; Mark Hadden: 106; david Frutos: 107; Ryuji Inoue: 108-109; C. Louisidis: 110-111; Image Courtesy SOM/© James Ewing | OTTO: 112; Stark Video Inc./Aerial New York © SOM: 113; Paul Ott: 114-115; Åke E:son Lindman: 116-117; Bo Bother/Laura Stamer: 118-119; Adam Mørk: 120-121; Jaklitsch/Gardner Architects: 122; CetraRuddy Architecture: 123; ArchSD, HKSARG: 124-125; PWP Landscape Architecture: 126; Halkin Mason Photography: 127; Amir Korour: 128-129; Don Weinreich/Ennead Architects: 130; Tabanlioglu Architects: 131; Hufton+Crow: 132 (tl, tr, cl, cr, br); Tim Snoek: 132 (bl); Hufton+Crow: 133; Kerem Sanilman: 134-135; Tim Griffith Photography: 136-137; Scott McDonald: 138-139; Serge Hoeltschi: 140; Gary Kessel: 141; Adria Goula: 142-143; Miran Kambic: 144-145; Andrew Rowat: 146-147; Alex Sutton: 148; SHoP Architects: 149; Bent René Synnevåg: 150-151; Anže ČOKL/Ofis: 152-153; Bruce Damonte: 154; John Gillooly: 155; SHoP Architects PC/WNYC: 156; People's Architecture office, Liqun Zhao: 157; Iwan Baan: 158-159; Bruce Engels: 160-161; Cao Pu/Cao Youtao: 162; McCall Burau: 163; Photos Courtesy of Silman: 164-165; Michael Law: 166 (cr, bl); Ramon Van der Heijden: 166 (t); Kevin NG: 166 (cl, br); Michael Law: 167; Luca Fortin: 168; damien murtagh: 169; Drew Echberg: 170-171; Jeremy Bitterman: 172-173; © Studio Dubuisson: 174-175; © Eric Staudenmaier: 176; Mariano Copete Franco/Francisco Chacón Martínez: 177; Downtown: 178; InTown Arquitetura: 179; Fernando Guerra | FG + SG: 180-181; Adam Goss, Red Mike, Ryan Clark: 182; Bjørn Leirvik: 183; Jaeyual Lee: 184-185; Rachel Brose/Thatcher Bean: 186-187; Albert Vecerka: 188-189; Petra Appelhof: 190-191; Florian Holzherr: 192-193; stør: 194-195; John Gollings (tl)(tr)(cl)(cr), Rory Daniel (b): 196; John Gollings: 197; Pavel Bendov Photography: 198-199; Michael Moran/OTTO: 200; © SOM/© ORNL: 201; Nguyen Tien Thanh: 202-203; Marcelo Villada Ortiz: 204-205; Yerçekim Photography: 206-207; Wang Ning: 208-209; Nart: 210-211; Siggen Stinessen: 212-213; Parham Taghioff: 214-215; Anice Hoachlander: 216; Paul Rivera: 217; Selim Erdil: 218-219; Naho Kubota: 220-221; Hufton + Crow (tr)(bl), Adam Mørk (tl)(c)(br): 222; Adam Mørk: 223; © Bruce Damonte/Olson Kundig: 224-225; michelle dunn: 226-227; Mecanoo: 228-229; Mahdi Fakhimi: 230; Adrian Gaut: 231; Edmund Sumner: 232-233; Yoshihiro Koitani: 234-235; Joe Fletcher Photography: 236 (tl, cl, cr, bl); Claudia Uribe Touri: 236 (tr); Claudia Uribe Touri: 237.